CHURCH COMES HOME

DAVE BARNHART
CHURCH COMES HOME

Start a House Church Network Anywhere

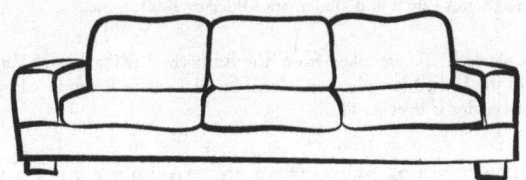

Nashville

CHURCH COMES HOME:
START A HOUSE CHURCH NETWORK ANYWHERE

Copyright © 2020 by Abingdon Press

All rights reserved.

No part of this work may be reproduced or transmitted in any form or by any means, electronic or mechanical, including photocopying and recording, or by any information storage or retrieval system, except as may be expressly permitted by the 1976 Copyright Act or in writing from the publisher. Requests for permission can be addressed to Permissions, Abingdon Press, 2222 Rosa L. Parks Boulevard, Nashville, TN 37228-1306, or permissions@abingdonpress.com.

Library of Congress Control Number: 2020941204
ISBN: 978-1-7910-0733-1

Scripture quotations unless noted otherwise are from the Common English Bible. Copyright © 2011 by the Common English Bible. All rights reserved. Used by permission. www.CommonEnglishBible.com.

Scripture quotations noted NRSV are taken from the *New Revised Standard Version of the Bible*, copyright 1989, Division of Christian Education of the National Council of the Churches of Christ in the United States of America. Used by permission. All rights reserved.

Scripture quotations marked (NIV) are taken from the Holy Bible, New International Version®, NIV®. Copyright © 1973, 1978, 1984, 2011 by Biblica, Inc.™ Used by permission of Zondervan. All rights reserved worldwide. www.zondervan.com The "NIV" and "New International Version" are trademarks registered in the United States Patent and Trademark Office by Biblica, Inc.™

Scripture quotations marked KJV are taken from The Authorized (King James) Version. Rights in the Authorized Version in the United Kingdom are vested in the Crown. Reproduced by permission of the Crown's patentee, Cambridge University Press.

20 21 22 23 24 25 26 27 28 29—10 9 8 7 6 5 4 3 2 1
MANUFACTURED IN THE UNITED STATES OF AMERICA

For all their uncompensated labor,
Like making coffee and biscuits
And tidying up on Sunday mornings
And reading all my stuff
And challenging my boneheaded ideas
And hugging me while I cry
And helping me deal with difficult people
And keeping me going
And being my team
And tolerating my moods
And sharing a mission
And making our home into a church
And our church into a home
And helping me maintain mostly healthy boundaries
This book is dedicated to Angela and Leo.

Let's go sailing this summer.

CONTENTS

ix — Preface
xi — House Church Quick Start Guide
xiii — Terms
xv — Introduction

Part One: Why Do House Church?

3 — Chapter 1. What Is a House Church?

15 — Chapter 2. Why House Church?

26 — Chapter 3. Principles of Organizing House Churches

Part Two: How Do We Start a House Church?

45 — Chapter 4. Assembling the First Group

51 — Chapter 5. Worship in House Churches

63 — Chapter 6. Discipleship and Leadership Development in House Churches

83 — Chapter 7. House Church Homiletics

89 — Chapter 8. Intergenerational Worship and Children in House Churches

94 — Chapter 9. Growing the Church and Spreading the Word

Contents

105 — Chapter 10. Group Dynamics in House Churches
110 — Chapter 11. Connecting House Churches
116 — Chapter 12. Oikonomics of House Churches
127 — Chapter 13. Future Possibilities for House Churches
131 — Bibliography

PREFACE

I submitted the completed manuscript for this book just as news was emerging that we might be facing a global pandemic. I did not expect that in a few months' time "house church" would take on a new and near-universal meaning as people self-isolated in their homes and started meeting online.

This illustrates an important new reality: we don't know yet what the outlines of church will look like in the light of climate change and a rapidly changing society. In *Parable of the Sower*, science fiction author Octavia Butler wrote, "God is change," and her theology is a challenge to a church that has historically emphasized stability and God's unchanging qualities. Pharaoh's Egypt and the Roman Empire were all about stability. The God of the Hebrews and of Jesus was about liberation, healing, and justice.

The church of the future must organize itself to be about the work of liberation, healing, and justice. This book is about one way to organize it.

HOUSE CHURCH QUICK START GUIDE

Unlike new phones or furniture, human communities do not come with a manual, but they are just as complicated, buggy, and difficult to assemble! We often start doing something and then refer to the manual only when we run into trouble. This Quick Start Guide is intended to give you an overview of some basic steps to assemble a house church, so you can see if you're missing any components or important steps. It can also help you explain to potential participants what a house church is.

You'll Need These Tools to Get Started

- A core group of three committed households (includes single individuals or families).

- One host or venue with comfortable seating (may be a private home, restaurant, or public space).

- Bibles or Bible apps (requires phones or smart devices with an internet connection).

- Devotional book of choice (optional).[1]

---

1. For groups that are just starting out, I recommend Shane Claiborne, Jonathan Wilson-Hartgrove, and Enuma Okoro, *Common Prayer: A Liturgy for Ordinary Radicals* (Grand Rapids: Zondervan, 2010); see also http://commonprayer.net.

New Group Procedure

- Meet individually with the core group and assess their readiness and excitement to participate.

- Meet as a group for a trial period of four to six weeks and establish the worship structure and devotional practices you will follow together.

- At the end of the trial period, invite the core group to make an eight- to twelve-month commitment to meet for worship and prayer.

- As a group, determine your spiritual direction and themes for the coming year.

- Be aware it may take eight to twelve months before your group ever has its first guest.

- Repeat often the importance of simplicity, discipleship, mission, and replication.

- Pray!

Organic Reproduction

When someone feels led to start a new house church, or the opportunity presents itself in another way (someone relocates, for example):

- Choose a new core team for the new house church with the new leader. It is especially useful here to reach out to new folks.

- Celebrate the birth of the new group.

- Give the parent group the opportunity to take "maternity leave." It may be helpful to take a couple of months off and reboot the parent group. Let everyone grieve the loss of old members.

- Follow the above New Group Procedure for the new group.

TERMS

Some of the terms I use in this book are used differently by different authors, and some may be unfamiliar to you.

Legacy church: a worshiping community whose primary gathering happens in a dedicated building. Legacy churches often have a variety of programs and ministries that operate on Sundays and during the week. Most have at least a part-time professional clergyperson but may have many staff and clergy at multiple campuses.

Traditional church or traditional worship service: a church whose worship is characterized by new and classic hymns, a sermon, forward-facing pews, and often an order of worship.

Contemporary church or contemporary worship service: a church whose worship is characterized by music with electronic instruments (guitars, keyboards, drums), projection screens, and possibly other creative multimedia elements. Sermons are usually still the focal point, although there is often more emphasis on the music than in traditional services.

House church: a worshiping community whose primary gathering happens in a private home or public space that is not primarily a worship space. There may or may not be a sermon. There may or may not be music. Prayer, conversation, sacrament, and the act of hospitality itself may be emphasized more than sermon or music.

Small group: part of a legacy church or a house church that does not necessarily meet for worship but for Bible study, accountability, service, social activities, special teaching, activism and advocacy, or other church activities outside of worship.

Intentional (Christian) community: groups of disciples who follow Jesus by living together and holding one another accountable to a community standard. These may be co-living residential arrangements (where people literally live in the same house, same neighborhood, or on the same land) or nonresidential arrangements (where people come together regularly, often more than once a week). Intentional communities share community practices like prayer and meditation, common meals, sustainable agriculture, or holding property in common. Though there are many forms of intentional community and some are nonreligious, when I use the term in this book it will refer to intentional Christian community.

Community organizing: the process of identifying the needs of a marginalized or oppressed community and developing the power to meet those needs through deep listening, leadership development, direct action, and policy change. Labor organizers and neighborhood activists are examples of community organizers.

Institutional church: a very broad term that indicates the organizing and administrative leadership of church systems. There is not one "thing" anyone can point to as the institutional church. It includes denominational bodies and nondenominational megachurches, seminaries and places of higher education, traditional and contemporary churches, publishers, consultants, and related businesses. House churches and intentional communities, being less formal and often operating outside of these formal leadership structures, are sometimes contrasted with "the institutional church."

INTRODUCTION

Two Prophetic Encounters

"I believe we could run the church better than the adults," I said to Eddie Johnson. Eddie was the youth minister in our local church, and I was fifteen. I don't remember exactly what about the adult church had irked me. I think I was the youth representative at some committee meeting. It was not the first time an idealistic teenager had made such a statement.

Eddie did not argue with me. Instead, he cast me in a play called *The First Church of Pete's Garage*.[1] The premise of the play is that the teenagers go off and start their own church. Along the way, because they are flawed human beings, the teenagers replicate all of the problems of the grown-up church. Pete learns that church is messy, leading is hard, and it's only by grace and the love of Christ that we can function as a community at all.

It's thirty years later, and I have to keep learning the same lessons. I've started quite a few house churches. A few have even persisted! Perhaps my youth minister had a spiritual gift of seeing the future, or perhaps he could simply see my passion. I'd always felt church could and should be fundamentally different.

Another story: Several years ago, I was commiserating with a friend about the decline of the institutional church, and he also spoke to me prophetically: "When was the last time you went to a record store?"

---

1. Paul McCusker, *The First Church of Pete's Garage* (Quincy, MA: Baker's Plays, 1982).

Introduction

I remember resenting the question. "Church is nothing like a record store," I replied. People come to a church for corporate worship, to experience God in community. We have a theological word for it: incarnational, the Word being made flesh. They experience the presence of Christ in a body of people. Dietrich Bonhoeffer referred to the sermon as the moment when Christ walks again among the congregation.[2] It cheapens the idea of church to talk about it as if it's a place you go to consume, to buy and possess music.

At the same time, I realized I couldn't answer the question. I don't remember the last time I went to a record store.

I do remember the experience of going. Compact discs were still sold in oversized boxes so that they would fit in displays meant for vinyl records. You could drop forty dollars in 1986 money on just two CDs. Prices on records and cassette tapes had plummeted, so I could walk out of the store with deals on oldies. I remember the anticipation of bringing the music home to listen to it.

Now, most of my music exists in the cloud, out in the ether somewhere. Some musicians thrive in this new environment by making a direct connection with their fan base.[3] Today, new talent often emerges not by being "discovered" by major recording labels but by sharing their songs on YouTube or SoundCloud. This approach doesn't necessarily make it easier to make a living with music. Many artists talk about how they receive only pennies in royalties from streaming services, in spite of massive listening audiences.

The internet has affected the church industry in the same way it has affected the music industry. Some voices are magnified while others are stifled. Some religious professionals make a comfortable living, and others struggle for love of their mission. The way people live and interact socially about their faith has changed. Phyllis Tickle spoke of a "rummage sale" that happens approximately every five hundred years in which our

---

2. Dietrich Bonhoeffer, *Worldly Preaching: Lectures on Homiletics* (New York: Crossroads, 1991), 101.

3. See Amanda Palmer, "The Art of Asking," *TED2013* (February 13, 2013), https://www.ted.com/talks/amanda_palmer_the_art_of_asking.

society reevaluates old ideas and develops new ways of seeing.[4] The last of these tectonic shifts happened when Gutenberg invented the printing press and it changed our relationship to the written word and to one another.

Failing Fast

I want to tell you about what happened when I started a church with the vision to reach the "nones and dones," those who report no primarily religious affiliation on surveys or consider themselves ex-churchgoers.

I failed.

Well, I failed to start a church that looked like the picture in my head. I had read a ton of books on church planting, on leadership, on strategy, on demographics, on evangelism, and on missions. I attended church planter boot camp and conferences on church growth. I listened to consultants and coaches. We started a church in 2013.

We wrote a lot of original music because the folks we were trying to reach were not turned on to either praise music or traditional hymns. We met in a bar. I preached my heart out with short, relevant, amazing sermons (if I do say so myself). We addressed timely topics and controversial issues that even edgy churches approach with caution. And we reached a lot of nones and dones who came to our worship services.

But they didn't stay.

I was perplexed, because sometimes these folks would shake my hand after a service and tell me how much they had loved the worship service, how exciting this concept was, and how they had never heard the Bible this way before. And then I would never see them again.

If you make it your mission to reach people who have given up on church, you have chosen a hard mission field. Possibly the hardest. It's like deciding to sell bacon to vegetarians: they don't particularly care for the flavor, and they're pretty sure it might kill them. And generally, they are correct about this last part.

---

4. Phyllis Tickle, *The Great Emergence: How Christianity Is Changing and Why* (Grand Rapids: Baker, 2008).

Introduction

I remember one conversation I had in a coffee shop with someone I had invited to church. He was a middle-aged gay man who had given up on church years before. He said, "I love what you're doing. I love the concept. I love your ministry and the way you preach the gospel. I am never going to church again in my life. But I am so grateful you are doing what you are doing."

I had to go through some intense reflection and personal spiritual work. I was disappointed with my inability to create the church I had in my head. I felt that I had let God down. Or maybe God had let me down. Or maybe my theology was wrong, or I wasn't called to reach the people I thought I was called to reach. Of course, my rational brain knew that success isn't a perfect indicator of good theology or of calling, and I had chosen a difficult mission field. But there's a difference between head knowledge and heart knowledge.

The place in our ministry where we had the most sticking power, the place where people's lives were most enriched, was in small groups. People valued the sense of community and friendships they developed. But the place I was pouring most of my energy was into worship—in music, in setting up the space each week, in sermon preparation and event planning. I was inadvertently following an "attractional" model of church, one where we asked people to come to an event, instead of a "missional" one where we discipled people and sent them out into the world. Two years into the planting process, I realized we needed a different approach.

That's how we stumbled into doing house church. House churches have been around from the beginning of Christianity, of course, and there have been several waves of house church movements as alternatives to legacy (or "institutional") churches.

This is the point where you may expect me to say that house churches turned everything around, that their viral growth power gave us a new sense of missional vitality, and that we've planted a network of organically reproducing, life-changing house churches that have reached thousands of people for Christ and have changed the culture of hundreds of neighborhoods. That hasn't happened quite yet. While I think that it is certainly a possibility and see huge opportunity for house churches in our culture, I am not only skeptical of these kinds of claims, I am not even sure that's the way God actually works. While I believe in a God who changes lives, sometimes dramatically and supernaturally, the God who let the Israelites wander forty years in the desert often works on longer time lines and through more natural processes. House churches are not a quick fix for what ails the church in North America.

What I will tell you instead is that I am convinced of the power and potential of house churches to reach people that legacy churches cannot. They can help people move toward greater intentional community, where church becomes not an event we attend, but an alternative society in which we live. For some, house churches may be an incremental step to an entirely different way of embodying Christian community, or a temporary step on the way back to a legacy church. For others, they may be the church.

I will also say that for denominational leaders and churches interested in reaching new people, house churches are a fantastic way to "fail fast" at church planting. Fail fast is a philosophy from digital business—and also from nature—that says it is better to try something, fail, and make incremental improvements than to wait for perfection to act. It presumes a fast-changing environment where leaders' agility is one of their most important assets.

Leadership gurus talk about this environment and leadership style as chaordic: a space on the frontier between very ordered structures and chaotic circumstances.[5] Much of the advice about chaordic leadership is about unlearning the top-down superior-subordinate leadership styles of our industrial past and embracing less hierarchical, more distributed forms of leadership. Especially in established denominations, churches tend to be highly structured, with lots of rules for how things are done properly. House churches are perched on the chaordic edge of the religious structures of the past, the free-for-all spiritual marketplace of the present, and whatever will emerge in the future.

---

5. Dee Hock, "The Art of Chaordic Leadership," *Leader to Leader Institute*, no. 15 (Winter 2000), http://www.griequity.com/resources/integraltech/GRIBusinessModel/chaordism/hock.html.

Introduction

This Book

I believe *decentralized networks of house churches—based on the principles of community organizing—are going to be a necessary survival strategy* for the church for the coming century. I will share more about this in the last chapter of this book.

This book is both a "why do?" and a "how to." The first three chapters deal with the heady stuff, about why we do house churches at all—about history, theology, and missiology; about how house churches address the particular needs of changing society; and how house churches fit into an ecosystem that contains both legacy churches and denominational structures. The rest of the book deals with the nuts and bolts of starting house churches, networking them together, and doing the daily business of ministry and discipleship. The last chapter is about how house churches will carry the ministry and mission of Jesus Christ forward into the next century.

I offer these lessons as a field researcher. I recognize that you may have a different theology and a different perspective, and may reach different conclusions than the lessons I draw from my experiences and research. I try to be descriptive rather than prescriptive, to share observations and recommendations rather than my opinions on how we should do church.

And I make these qualifying statements because one of the core principles of house church is that leadership and expertise are shared. When a pastor sits as one among many in a circle, instead of standing in the front and preaching to an audience, the dynamic changes. It is the wisdom of the group that mediates the voice of the Holy Spirit, not the preacher. The church itself speaks back to the preacher, and there are sometimes holy moments when I recognize God's voice speaking from the margins, when a child asks a question or a newcomer finds their voice and adds to the conversation.

In the same way, I recognize that my voice is one in the circle. I believe I bring an important perspective that connects the institutional church with community organizing and with a population of people who are done with church. But there are people who have been doing house churches longer, especially outside the umbrella of a denominational body, who have far more experience than me among different populations.

If there is a house church revolution taking shape, it will not be because a celebrity preacher announces it. It will happen because of the collective action and wisdom of laypeople and humble clergy who are in tune with the good news and the wisdom of the Holy Spirit, who recognize, in the words of the children's song, "The church is not a building . . . the church is a people!"[6]

---

6. Richard K. Avery and Donald S. Marsh, "We Are the Church," *The United Methodist Hymnal* (Nashville: United Methodist Publishing House, 1995), no. 558.

PART ONE
WHY DO HOUSE CHURCH?

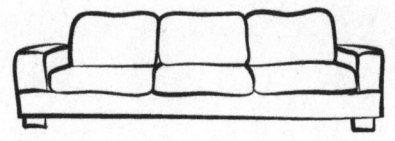

CHAPTER 1
WHAT IS A HOUSE CHURCH?

The First Three Questions

If you tell someone you are part of a house church, there are three questions you will likely be asked:

1. "Is that . . . like . . . a real church?"
2. "Do you have . . . you know . . . a real preacher?"
3. "Are you part of a cult?"

I love these questions. I've heard some version of them whenever I introduce the concept of house churches to people who are not familiar with them.

Not only are these questions blunt and honest but they also reflect the same skepticism I used to have about house churches. I'd grown up in traditional United Methodist churches, and had served churches ranging from less than a hundred to several thousand. All had buildings and at least one full-time staff person. While I was aware of the existence of house churches, and while I had heard occasionally about the "house church movement" at various times in my ministry, I remained skeptical. Though I would not have said so explicitly, I thought of churches with buildings and large staff as "real" churches.

3

The pastoral journey I've been on for the last several years as a planter and leader of house churches has forced me to wrestle with each of these questions. It has challenged me and changed my practice and theory of ministry.

Of course, if someone had asked me these questions about house churches years ago, I could have given the "right" answers to these questions, historically and theologically. These are short answers I'd learned in seminary and Bible study:

"Is that . . . like . . . a real church?"

Here is my *historical answer*: For the first three hundred years of its existence, the church met almost exclusively in people's homes. Paul's letters are addressed to churches that meet in homes. So if those were real churches, modern house churches are real churches.

Here is my *theological answer*: Jesus says that wherever two or more are gathered in his name, he is present (Matthew 18:20). Any small gathering of Jesus-followers is a "real" church.

"Do you have . . . you know . . . a real preacher?"

Historical answer: We think of Paul as a real preacher and pastor, even though he moved around a lot and had a day job as a tentmaker (Acts 18:1-4).

Theological answer: The ministry of the church is carried out by all baptized believers, not just the preachers or pastors. In our case, yes, we do have an ordained pastor as a leader, but the pastor doesn't make a church "real."

"Are you part of a cult?"

Historical answer: House churches have been around since the earliest days of the church and continue to be the primary form of church in many parts of the world. People who are not part of a house church often regard them with suspicion, especially in places like China, where it benefits the powerful to portray house churches as dangerous.

What Is a House Church?

Theological answer: Nearly all genuine movements of the Holy Spirit have been called "cults" at some point, and their leaders portrayed as heretics. Anabaptists were persecuted in France, and Martin Luther was threatened in Germany. John Wesley was forbidden to preach in his church, and so preached outside. Jesus actually told his followers to expect to be called devils by religious authorities (Matthew 10:25). So, no, we are not a cult; we are a manifestation of the grand tradition of reformation and transformation through church history.

These are fine answers, and I will explore each of them in greater detail later in this book. But there is a difference between "knowing the right answer" because you learned it in Bible study or seminary and *knowing it in your bones*. I knew all of these answers before, and I *still* harbored a prejudice that house churches were not "real church." Sometimes we talk about the difference between "head knowledge" (theoretical, whether abstract or specific), "heart knowledge" (intuited and believed), and "embodied knowledge" (lived and experienced). Leading house churches has helped me move this knowledge from my head into my heart and my body.[1]

Taken together, all three of these questions ask a larger implicit question about *legitimacy* and *authenticity*: Who or what grants authority for doing church in this way? And is it trustworthy—to members, to the larger global church, and to the community "outside" of the church?

The only way to answer this implicit question is with more questions: Does this church change lives? Does it convince people who are not part of it that it has something worthy to offer the world? Is it faithful to the good news and legacy of Jesus Christ, and does it stand in relation to two thousand years of Christian history in some way that makes it recognizable as "church"?

I assume, if you're reading this book, that you are already intrigued by the idea of house churches, and that you may have some familiarity with the historical and theological basis for doing house church. But I also

---

1. The next level of knowledge is moving it from our own heads, hearts, and bodies into the life of the community—which is also part of the house church model. It's easy for pastors to forget that it is one thing for the pastor to know something, and quite another for the church to live it out.

recognize that in North America, house churches are often perceived as a fringe or niche ministry. You may be skeptical, as I used to be, of the legitimacy or effectiveness of house churches. I now believe that house churches are not only legitimate and effective forms of ministry, but that they are vital in both senses of the word—as "necessity" and as "life-giving"—in the twenty-first century.

Denominational leaders are beginning to recognize house churches as an important tool in their ministry toolbox, in addition to legacy churches and other nontraditional Christian communities. Church planters who may have thought of house churches as a temporary arrangement on the way to "real" church are recognizing house churches as ends in themselves instead of stepping stones to something better. Scholars in the sociology of religion, in homiletics, and in evangelism are studying house churches. And community organizers and activists see the power and possibility in house churches to create social change.

Defining House Church

The definition of house church varies widely among people who study church. Luther Smith includes house churches as one form of "intentional community," those groups of "Christian disciples who are dissatisfied with any traditions and forms of organization that do not empower them to respond fully to God's call." These groups who start alternative churches, new monastic groups, base communities, or house churches "labor for a fellowship of intimacy, where members nurture and care for each other's physical, emotional, and spiritual needs" as well as "mission, where compassion for God's people involves the fellowship in social action."[2]

While Smith casts a large net and includes house churches among many different kinds of intentional community, some who study house churches narrow the scope and definition. J. D. Payne, author of *Missional House Churches*, seeks to distinguish between what he believes are biblical, evangelical house churches and other forms that might be, for him, too liberal or ineffective. While I do not agree with Payne's theology, I find

---

2. Luther Smith, *Intimacy and Mission: Intentional Community as Crucible for Radical Discipleship* (Eugene, OR: Wipf and Stock, 1994), 22.

his observations about house churches to be insightful and helpful. Payne makes a distinction between house churches, which have a high degree of autonomy, and cell churches, which are semiautonomous but are part of a larger church. He also distinguishes between missional house churches, which are outwardly focused on spreading the gospel and baptizing new believers, and inwardly focused house churches, which have become a haven for griping about the institutional church.

Our network would probably fit what Payne calls "cell churches," instead of house churches, since we have many networked house churches, but we have the name of one church (Saint Junia), share one treasury, and share one full-time pastor. We make leadership decisions as a large group. We certainly have much in common with "cells," especially yeast, because each house church is intended to bud and produce more house churches. But this term is too easily confused with "cell groups," which are often simply a program of a larger legacy church. Our vision for house churches is that they are lay-led, decentralized, disciple-making communities.

In every house church that we start, I make it clear to the participants that they are free to be as much a part of the network as they want to be. If, at some point, under the direction of the Holy Spirit, a house church decided to become completely autonomous, I would not consider that a loss. This is exactly how a yeast cell multiplies, by budding and sometimes separating! But I feel this distinction about autonomy is too rigid. What connects our house churches is not a hierarchical structure, but a set of shared practices and mission.

Tony and Felicity Dale, along with George Barna, classify house churches as one form of "simple church." They found that in 2008, six million adults attended some form of simple church each week.[3] In both Payne's and Barna's research, they point out that surveying and counting how many house churches actually exist in North America is difficult, and that the numbers change depending on how you ask the question.

My definition of house church is broad and simple. It's also functional, not theological, because I recognize a huge, diverse set of practices

---

3. Tony Dale, Felicity Dale, and George Barna, *The Rabbit and the Elephant: Why Small Is the New Big for Today's Church* (Brentwood, TN: Barna, 2009), 28.

and beliefs as being legitimately Christian. My definition is *a church of two or more who meet regularly outside of a dedicated church building, and who consider that fellowship to be their spiritual home.*

Once we establish a definition of house churches, it is equally interesting how we define what remains. What do we call churches that have dedicated buildings and professional staff? Sometimes we use terms like "institutional church," "traditional church," or "conventional church." I generally avoid the term "traditional church," because it would be easy to think we're just talking about churches with high liturgy and hymnals, and not churches with stadium seating and big screens. I'm not crazy about the words *institutional* or *conventional* either, because I think the words often take on a negative connotation and ignore the rich, vibrant, organic life that can be present in such places. Also, even though I plant house churches, I am part of a denomination that is itself an institution. I value "institutional memory" and the institutional ways human beings organize complex structures. "Conventional" makes it sound like institutional churches aren't doing innovative ministry.

Tony and Felicity Dale prefer the term "legacy churches," recognizing their important, ongoing work of embodying one form of church life. This will be the term I use in this book to describe churches with dedicated buildings and professional staff.

The research reveals that most participants in house churches come from legacy churches, and most house churches are relatively young: 80 percent of the churches in the Payne study had been meeting for less than ten years.[4]

Are You Affiliated with a Denomination?

Sometimes people will ask if a house church is affiliated with a denomination. While ours is affiliated with The United Methodist Church, the majority of house churches are not affiliated.[5] For some people, part of the appeal of house churches is that they are free from bureaucratic struc-

---

4. J. D. Payne, *Missional House Churches: Reaching Our Communities with the Gospel* (Downers Grove, IL: InterVarsity, 2007), 50.

5. Payne, *Missional House Churches*, 64.

tures and hierarchies. House churches offer a way to avoid the politicking that happens in larger institutions, as well as the theological wrangling between polarized factions.

While Saint Junia chooses to remain affiliated with my denominational body, I support any expression of church that brings the good news to new audiences. The strength of house churches is their ability to embody an indigenous expression of church in a particular place or neighborhood. If your community tends to be conservative, your house church may be conservative. If it tends to be liberal, your house church may be liberal. There is even the possibility that we might actually sit down for a meal and have a theological disagreement across these dividing lines while remaining loving and respectful, and while we focus our attention on God and our neighbors.

For a house church, I have found that "brand recognition" is both a strength and a weakness of denominational affiliation. Some people—even some who are generally suspicious of institutions!—give greater legitimacy to house churches who are affiliated with a denomination. I've even had someone say to me, "Well, if you're Methodist, you must be legit." This may be because denominational affiliation offsets suspicions that a house church may be creepy or teach suspect theology.

Two of our recent members are sisters who told me that they "Facebook stalked" our house churches for six months before they eventually decided to try it out! They said, "We wanted to make sure you guys weren't some kind of cult." They also wanted to make sure our theology would not be oppressive to them.

House church enthusiasts often say that part of their philosophy is to get back to a way of doing church before denominations, before schisms and abstract theological arguments created insiders and outsiders, when following The Way of Jesus was about practice and a way of life instead of a set of beliefs to which we give our intellectual assent. For these enthusiasts, house churches are a way to do church "the way Jesus and the early church did it."

While I am sympathetic to this view and believe it reflects a good theology of how church *should* be, I do not consider it *historically* accurate.

Chapter 1

There are two thousand years of church history between us and Jesus: schisms and conflicts, saints and villains, and rooms and rooms full of books. When churches claim that they read the Bible the way Jesus did, or when they refuse to tell guests that their theology is closer to John Calvin's than Dorothy Day's, I find it dishonest. There is a reason and a history of why we do baptism a certain way,[6] or why churches do or do not ordain women,[7] or forbid or allow members to join the military.[8] Someone, somewhere in our two thousand-year history had a strong theological opinion, or preferred one practice to another, or read the Bible differently from their neighbor, and that informs how we practice now. We need to be honest about how we approach these questions. Being dismissive about them is often a way to bait-and-switch the theologically naive.

Since I do come from a denominational affiliation, I want to be clear about my own biases and beliefs. I refer to the two thousand-year history that all Jesus-followers share, which includes Roman Catholic hierarchy and Quaker egalitarianism, Greek Orthodox icons and Puritans who rejected them, Anabaptist reformers and Ethiopian and Coptic traditions, Latin American liberation theology and American evangelicalism. For people in the southeastern United States who have often grown up only hearing one version of conservative Christianity, I hope to wow participants with the diversity of belief and practice in God's big-*C* Church. I want them to have a buffet of religious tradition so that they understand there is more than one way to be the church. In this sense I do not want to be nondenominational but *trans*-denominational. Even though I am ordained by a denominational body, I want our house churches to embody an ecumenical future.

---

6. Descriptions of ancient baptism include a training period of three years. As for the ceremony, men and women were baptized separately. They disrobed and entered the baptismal pool nude (just as they were when they were born the first time) and received a new white robe when they emerged. There may be churches that still baptize this way in Alabama, but I'm pretty sure most of those that claim to be "just like the early church" do not.

7. How and to what extent women held pastoral leadership in the early church remains a point of contention among different Christian traditions today.

8. The *Didache* forbade military service or any profession that involved violence.

House churches turn out to be great places to have nondivisive conversations about these issues that have divided churches in the past. Because we are sitting in a circle, and because I as a leader do not have to have the last word, we can disagree about free will and predestination, or infant and believer's baptism, and why those disputes have mattered to churches. This is a way both to take seriously our two thousand–year shared history, and to relativize it according to our house churches' practices and mission. You are welcome in our house churches, for example, to disagree about whether the Bible permits women in leadership—but you aren't free to prevent women from leading.

What's Wrong with "Regular" Church?

This is a question I sometimes get when I tell people about house churches. I try to make it clear that I do not reject legacy churches. But there is no one-size-fits-all kind of church. The body of Christ has been incarnate in multiple places and multiple cultures. It has worshiped on every continent and even in space.[9] Legacy churches, no less than house churches, have their own role in giving glory to God, forming disciples, and spreading the good news. There are economies of scale and specific advantages that large churches and legacy churches have.

There are some motivating factors for people who choose house churches, though. Some simply dislike large crowds and prefer the intimacy of a house church. These folks are more common than you think! Some long for greater intimacy that they can have only in a smaller, committed community. Some are enchanted with the model of the church they read about in Acts, which met in homes and was more like an extended family than a corporation or activity center.

Quite a few prefer house churches because of church trauma—because their family and pastor used religion to shame them about their sexual orientation, or their choice of friends or vocation, or their interest in

---

9. Emily McFarlan Miller and Jack Jenkins, "5 Faith Facts about the Moon Landing: Space Communion and a Prayer League of Its Own," *National Catholic Reporter* (July 20, 2019), https://www.ncronline.org/news/people/5-faith-facts-about-moon-landing-space-communion-and-prayer-league-its-own.

science and evolution. They find that they are more able to be authentically themselves among a small group of disciples. They are better able to find healing and ways to reframe their faith in conversation, as opposed to hearing a man (and in their context it is usually a man) lecture them for half an hour.

Some find they are better able to live out the Bible's call to social justice in a smaller setting. Luther Smith observes that people choose intentional communities because the institutional church often "accommodates the values of the secular society." He continues:

> It develops theology and practices which endorse the materialism, nationalism, and social prejudices of the dominant culture. Often this means that the church fails to be an advocate for civil rights, the needs of the poor, justice for the oppressed, and peace between nations. To preserve the image of being a stable and affirming social institution, decisions about ministries are based on the principle that conflict must be held to a minimum, and that members should not be offended by controversial ministries.[10]

Still others find that house churches make evangelism seem both more natural and effective. Talking to someone about your faith feels more genuine when it feels more like a conversation and less like a recruitment program. Newcomers to house churches may be shocked to hear that their thoughts and experiences matter to the group.

I'll explore some of these in more detail in upcoming chapters, but the main point about legacy churches is this: Although there are legitimate theological and personal reasons why folks may choose to participate in house churches, house churches are not better or more authentically Christian than legacy churches. They are just different.

Even more important, in North America, most house churches emerge from legacy churches. Smith writes about the spiritual debt most members of intentional communities have to the legacy church:

> The institutional church, however, is more than the source of members' dissatisfaction. The church is also the alma mater of religious vi-

---

10. Smith, *Intimacy and Mission*, 19.

sion and ideals for Christian discipleship. Many members received their understanding of the Christian faith's radical message from institutional churches. Pulpits and Sunday school classes portrayed inspiring messages of Christians deeply involved with one another's lives and boldly engage in the social crises of God's world. The spiritual turmoil caused by churches whose witness retreated from enacting this radical message eventually led these members to seek another expression of God's church: intentional religious community.[11]

For many members, house churches are not a rejection of the institutional church or legacy churches. They are simply the next step of their discipleship journey as they answer a call to greater commitment that affects more areas of their lives. They are convinced that the good news requires them to open their homes to folks who might not otherwise step into a church sanctuary.

Indigenous and Tenacious Church

This is the lens through which I view the concept of house church: it is one model among many, and every house church is a new expression of the indigenous culture. Like a sower casting seed, a church planter can start many different house churches. Some may fail and some may thrive, depending on the soil in which they land, but there will be a harvest nonetheless. The planter of house churches focuses on practices, not programs, and developing a "staff" of lay leadership instead of professional full-time employees. House churches are like leaven, mustard weeds, or a virus: they stay simple in order to reproduce fast, instead of growing larger and more complex.

"Indigenous expression" means they adapt to the needs of the local community. Some house churches are centered around a common meal. Some are not. Some like singing. Some do not. Some have lots of kids who require us to find ways to incorporate them into worship. Others have few or no kids, or only require childcare during worship. House churches are hyperlocal. Saint Junia has one house church primarily composed of nurses and healthcare workers who work weekends, and so preferred a

---

11. Smith, *Intimacy and Mission*, 79.

non-singing weekday night worship time. One is made up mostly of black LGBTQ members who make eating dinner part of their Sunday afternoon tradition. Another house church is made up mainly of parents of kids between the ages of eight and eleven, whose kids need their own time of spiritual education. Each of these has different needs and slightly different cultural expectations of what church is supposed to be.

My hope, in this polarized society in the first half of the twenty-first century, is that if people feel alienated from legacy churches due to theology, politics, prejudice, or church polity, they will not simply drop out, but will organize to create new churches. One of the characteristics of life is that it is tenacious; it takes advantage of a changing environment. When forests burn, opportunistic seeds and spores take advantage of the soft ash and open canopy. When drought strikes or food gets scarce, some animals hibernate and some plants change their growth strategy. Life is so tenacious that we even find life thriving near volcanic vents at the bottom of the sea floor.

The church is going through its own set of disasters: polarization, declining social participation, sexual misconduct, clergy scandals, schism, and a long-overdue reckoning with racism. All of these disasters also present opportunities. Historically, schism has been a catalyst for evangelistic growth. There are many people who are hungry for good news that is really good news, and plenty of denominational bodies have a viable structure, missional history, and disciple-making paradigm that could make house churches a powerful witness in the next century. Instead of bemoaning the social forces that make life hard for the institutional church, we can look with excitement at the new forms of church life this new world can grow.

CHAPTER 2
WHY HOUSE CHURCH?

Growing Like a Weed

He continued, "What's a good image for God's kingdom? What parable can I use to explain it? Consider a mustard seed. When scattered on the ground, it's the smallest of all the seeds on the earth; but when it's planted, it grows and becomes the largest of all vegetable plants. It produces such large branches that the birds in the sky are able to nest in its shade."
—Mark 4:30-32

I need to point out the obvious: a mustard plant is not a cedar tree.

Jesus's original audience would have heard the reference. "The birds of the air" and their nest-making comes from a passage in Ezekiel. It described how Israel was like a tender cutting from a cedar tree, planted on the top of Mount Zion.

> On the mountain heights of Israel I will plant it; it will produce branches and bear fruit and become a splendid cedar. Birds of every kind will nest in it; they will find shelter in the shade of its branches. (Ezekiel 17:23 NIV)

Both Matthew and Luke struggle a bit with this parable. Each says that the mustard turns into a tree, which is where we expect birds to make their nests. Mark's Jesus says it is a shrub, and ground-dwelling birds make nests in its shade.

I've heard this parable preached about how small things become great, how small churches become big, how the kingdom grows from tiny beginnings but becomes huge. I read from a different perspective. Jesus's audience expected to be told that Israel would be made great again, but Jesus seems to indicate that they should not expect a tall and majestic cedar tree. They should be thinking of a shrub.

Mustard, by the way, could be a nuisance. Pliny the Elder said, "It grows entirely wild, though it is improved by being transplanted; but on the other hand when it has once been sown, it is scarcely possible to get the place free of it, as the seed when it falls germinates at once."[1]

The growth Jesus talks about is not visually impressive, but it is tenacious. I imagine if he were to tell the same parable to a North American audience, he might say that the Kingdom of God is more like a dandelion than a chestnut tree, more like kudzu than an oak. I take inspiration from this parable that the church should be something that reproduces rapidly, that puts less energy into becoming big and more energy into becoming contagious. Viral, even.

We have modern parables that say something similar. Tony and Felicity Dale, writing with George Barna, suggest that churches should be more like rabbits than like elephants.[2] Put two elephants in a room, they say, and two years later you may have three elephants. Put two rabbits in a room, though, and in two years there will be more rabbits than you can count! The gestational period for a baby elephant is more than a year, and elephants take a long time to grow to reproductive maturity. Rabbits, on the other hand, breed like . . . well, rabbits. In the same way, they argue, churches should be less focused on growing their size and more on reproducing churches.

Another similar parable about growth and reproduction is found in the title of a book by Ori Brafman and Rod Beckstrom: *The Starfish and the Spider: The Unstoppable Power of Leaderless Organizations*.[3] Some star-

---

1. Quoted in Amy-Jill Levine, *Short Stories by Jesus: The Enigmatic Parables of a Controversial Rabbi* (New York: Harper Collins, 2014), 160. Levine is skeptical of the mustard-as-weed theory, but I am following David Buttrick's interpretation in David Buttrick, *Speaking Parables: A Homiletic Guide*, 1st ed. (Louisville: Westminster John Knox, 2000). I think Jesus's sayings were retold and written down, in part, because they challenged triumphalistic theology.

2. See Dale, Dale, and Barna, *The Rabbit and the Elephant*.

3. Ori Brafman and Rod A. Beckstrom, *The Starfish and the Spider: The Unstoppable Power of Leaderless Organizations* (New York: Portfolio, 2006).

fish, if they are cut into pieces, simply regrow into more starfish. One starfish that undergoes the trauma of being chopped up may become five new starfish! This is how the book of Acts described the church responding under persecution. When Stephen is killed (Acts 8:1-8), the church in Jerusalem scatters to new locations, where it continues to grow.

A starfish's relatively simple structure and lack of specialized body parts mean that it is hard to kill by dismemberment. Brafman and Beckstrom describe starfish-like organizations as those that have the following characteristics: they lack a single person in charge and have no headquarters, they can survive a "thump on the head," they do not have many specialized roles and do not have to communicate through intermediaries, and they are self-funding. Many legacy organizations, though, more closely resemble spiders: they have a high degree of complexity, cannot survive dismemberment, and if "thumped on the head" cannot recover.

I believe this decentralized, fast-reproducing, tenacious life is the kind of growth Jesus describes in his parable as *mustard seed growth*. It is exactly the opposite of what many church planters and pastors are taught to consider success. We have been taught that a big church is a successful church. I have heard countless church-planting stories about how a church started with eight people around a dinner table and became a thousand-member church within three years. We don't tell stories about how a church started with eight people around a dinner table and three years later was a different set of people around two or three different dinner tables.

Dying Like a Weed

Here's another harsh reality about mustard: it is an annual, not a perennial. Unlike a cedar, it will not live decades. It is not meant to. It will live for a season, not for centuries. Mustard's long-term survival strategy lies in its ability to reproduce. Cedar is known for its ability to resist rot and is used to build things. A mustard church, though, is not focused on long-term sustainability, but on thriving in the now.

When we talk about starting churches, a big question for those investing time and resources in them is often sustainability. The expectation is that a church, once started, should last for years and years. It needs to become self-sustaining financially and structurally. From an institutional perspective, "sustainability" is usually defined as the ability to support a full-time professional staff or clergy person and upkeep on a building. This is one major reason, I think, that house churches have not been a major focus of denominations. It's also why most church-planting has been done in new suburbs, where money is more plentiful and stability easier to achieve, than in poor neighborhoods or rural areas.

In his study of missional house churches, J. D. Payne found that 80 percent had been meeting for less than ten years.[4] While this shows that house churches grow and spread fast, it may also be evidence that house churches tend to live fast and die young. House church guru Frank Viola says that the average life cycle for a house church is about six months to four years.[5] My own experience is that the survival rate of house churches over four years is about fifty percent.

This short life cycle points to another difference between cedar and mustard: the primary purpose of mustard for humans is to give zest and flavor to life. In this way, it is a bit like Jesus's famous description of his followers: we are like salt (Matthew 5:13). Disciples are supposed to be zesty! By contrast, we use cedar structurally. We use it to build. In the lands of the Bible, because trees have been scarce for thousands of years, cedar is still a luxury building item. Cedar and mustard have very different uses, just as legacy churches and house churches have different uses.

I want to reiterate: a mustard-weed church is not meant to give long-term structural stability to social systems. It is meant to make disciples more zesty!

North American Christians have a tendency to read the parables, like the rest of the Bible, through a triumphalistic lens, where bigger is better, where wealth indicates success, and where success is ordained by God. These North American notions of greatness contradict the theology of the cross and a God who chooses to be incarnate not at the top of a hierarchy, but at the bottom. Mustard is not cedar.

---

4. Payne, *Missional House Churches*, 50.

5. Frank Viola, *So You Want to Start a House Church? First-Century Styled Church Planting for Today* (Gainesville, FL: Present Testimony Ministry, 2003), 117.

Mustard-weed churches affirm that God's action of saving the world is consistently bottom-up, not top-down. God may anoint kings in order to satisfy our craving for authority, but prefers principled anarchy to monarchy, and liberators (judges) to kings (1 Samuel 8). God chooses a poet to kill a giant (1 Samuel 17). God chooses shepherds and foreigners rather than clergy to herald the birth of Jesus (Luke 2:8-20; Matthew 2:1-12). When speaking truth to power, God picks Amos, a bi-vocational farmer, rather than a full-time, professional, court-appointed prophet (Amos 7:10-17). House churches witness to God's action at the grass roots.

This doesn't mean there isn't a place for legacy churches, or megachurches, or full-time professional clergy. It just means that in the ecosystem of God's saving activity, there is more than one strategy at work.

I could be wrong, of course. I don't know for certain if this is what Jesus was getting at with his parable of the mustard seed. But if I'm listening to Jesus and expecting cedar, and instead he gives me mustard, then I suspect that our notions of the kingdom need to be recalibrated. Ada María Isasi-Díaz even takes it a step further by shifting the metaphor from "kingdom" to something less hierarchical: "kin-dom," God's family, where we stop striving to be greatest and relate to one another as siblings.[6] Part of what Jesus was doing with this parable, and part of what the church needs to be doing, is recalibrating our notions of greatness and bigness: "Those who are last will be first" (Matthew 20:16).

Mustard is my biblical and theological reason for doing house church. But there are practical needs that house churches can meet that are unique to our time and place. These include individual, institutional, and social needs.

Individual Needs: To Make Disciples

Loneliness is a public health crisis.[7] The health effects of loneliness have been compared to smoking fifteen cigarettes a day, and they impact

---

6. Ada María Isasi-Díaz, *Mujerista Theology: A Theology for the Twenty-First Century* (Maryknoll, NY: Orbis Books, 1996).

7. Kerstin Gerst-Emerson and Jayani Jayawardhana, "Loneliness as a Public Health Issue: The Impact of Loneliness on Health Care Utilization among Older Adults," *American Journal of Public Health* 105, no. 5 (2015), 1013–19. https://doi.org/10.2105/AJPH.2014.302427, https://www.ncbi.nlm.nih.gov/pmc/articles/PMC4386514/.

mental health and longevity.[8] Although the internet has revolutionized communication, and although we are more "connected" to one another than ever before through social media, many of us experience social isolation and crippling loneliness. It is a spiritual epidemic.

Some of this is not unique to our time and place, of course. While I would be as excited as any good sci-fi fan if we discovered signals from alien life in outer space, there is something ironic about our species of seven billion humans, living among countless amazing animal and plant species, scanning the stars and asking, "Are we alone in the universe?" We seem to think discovering alien life would make us feel less alone, but I suspect that it would simply let us feel alone together. Our loneliness is not assuaged by our connectivity or our proximity, the number of species on our planet or among the stars. Our communication technologies only amplify our existential loneliness, stoke our fear of missing out, and confirm the notion that other people are living much more emotionally rich lives than we are.

House churches are well equipped to address people's existential loneliness, both by providing a place in which people can be vulnerable with one another during worship and by inoculating them against loneliness during the week. It helps me to reframe my thinking if someone shared on Sunday morning or Tuesday night that there's nothing abnormal about my negative feelings. Connecting with others in deep ways makes my alone time more rich and fulfilling. Dietrich Bonhoeffer observed that our time alone prepares us to be with others, and our time with others prepares us to be alone.[9]

Discipleship is not primarily about training people to be active in an organization, but forming them for life in the Kin-dom even while our society is actively resisting it. Jesus taught the disciples he gathered around himself to live as an extended family, even referring to them as his siblings (Mark 3:34). House churches help us to recognize our existential loneliness, the ways our society contributes to it, and how we can live out a new way of being in relation to one another.

---

8. Claire Pomeroy, "Loneliness Is Harmful to Our Nation's Health," *Scientific American* (March 20, 2019), https://blogs.scientificamerican.com/observations/loneliness-is-harmful-to-our-nations-health/.

9. Dietrich Bonhoeffer, *Life Together* (San Francisco: HarperSanFrancisco, 1993), 55.

Disciples are those who are growing in love of God and of their neighbors by following Jesus. We often talk about the church's responsibility to make disciples, but we don't often address people's *need to be disciples*. Discipleship is what we need. We are built to be in relationship with one another and God.

Institutional Needs: To Grow the Church

The institutional church is well aware of the many crises it faces. "Change or die" has been the mantra for decades, yet the number of nones and dones continues to grow while church participation shrinks. It is clear that this is not simply a marketing problem, but a systemic and spiritual problem. While we have no end of motivational change agents and celebrity preachers encouraging us to innovate to reach new demographics, the usual recommendations for solving church decline amount to "love Jesus more and try harder."

We live in an age in which people distrust all institutions: government, media, business, and certainly the church. To survive, much less grow, the institutional church needs to rediscover its noninstitutional nature.

A word of clarification here: I love institutions. I think they are spiritual, though not always in the ways they intend. I love the many ways human beings organize their activity together. And I love the institutional church. I love denominations and their Byzantine policies and their many different names for the same thing (district, parish, synod, conference, assembly). I do not think it is possible to say "I love human beings" without loving the way they organize their social lives, without marveling at the wisdom of groups and how we develop processes to allocate resources and talent. It's like saying "I love bees" but hating the hives they live in, or "I love coral" but hating reefs.

Yet churches cannot understand themselves primarily as institutions or as businesses who recruit members or clients. Evangelism cannot be advertising. Churches are supposed to be an alternative community to the dominant culture, and the good news is that Christ is actually alive, present, and working in the people among you. It's hard to affirm that reality when our organizational life has an administrative board that follows Robert's Rules of Order, and when a significant amount of what we call "ministry" is event planning and mass mailings. Institutional church life in America does not look significantly different from the rest of our culture. Luther Smith writes:

> Would a visitor to my church—after seeing how we relate to one another in our fellowship, attending a church business meeting, determining the commitments of our budget, or assessing our involvements in the society—better understand God's passion for love and justice?[10]

If those of us who have lived and breathed the institutional church for most of our lives have trouble answering yes, how much more so for the folks whose main experience of church has been what they consume from the news, or whose childhood and teenage experiences were mostly negative!

Though they often operate under the radar of the institutional church, house churches can be like spores that extend the church mycelium into hostile territory. Among people who are jaded about organized religion, these simply organized groups of friends can soften resistance to the gospel. House churches can help the institutional church by reminding people inside and outside the church of our roots. They are an extended family of people "called out" of the dominant culture to live in an alternative kin-dom.

There are people in our house churches who swore they would never set foot inside another church, who said they don't "do" organized religion, and who hadn't attended a worship service in years. There are far more people whom I know through social circles who tell me, "I don't go to church, but if I did, I would go to one of your house churches."

Social Needs: To Change the World

One celebrity preacher used to say that the local church is the hope of the world. I still believe it, even though he left ministry recently because of allegations of sexual harassment.

---
10. Smith, *Intimacy and Mission*, 18.

I have a hard time writing those words. This typifies the promise and the problem with the church—that the language of hope and salvation often goes hand-in-hand with the action of sin and abuse. I've heard more than a few preachers say that the church is God's Plan A of salvation, and that there is no Plan B. This kind of news makes me think God needs a better strategy.

Here's the slippery thing, though: Christians have forever distinguished between the *visible* church and the *invisible* church. The early church called themselves the *ekklesia*, which in Greek means the *called-out ones*. It was a better description than "kicked out," which was also true: they were kicked out of religious communities and often also their families. There are many in our culture who are the kicked-out ones, or who have suffered abuse at the hands of pastors and church people, who I hope find an adopted family who becomes church to them. In this way, those who leave the church *become* the church, the *ekklesia*. The *ekklesia*, by definition, is not a building or an institution.

The *ekklesia* expresses the heart of God: the last will be first, the prisoners will go free, the wounded will be healed, the creation will be made whole. Human beings and human community are methods the Holy Spirit uses to accomplish these purposes. When institutions fail to be the church—which happens so often—God is still God. And somewhere, outside of the institutions that often serve the powerful, kicked-out people rise up to be the *ekklesia* as God intended. This is why I still believe, in spite of so many things, that God continues to use the invisible church to work out salvation in this world. House churches are a signifier of that divine movement of moving outside in order to create a new inside, of intentionally moving toward those outside the walls. We move to the margins in order to find where Christ is truly the center.

It is completely possible, of course, for abuse and exclusion to manifest in house churches as well. Wherever we go, we carry human sin with us. But the *ekklesia* is always being called out into a wider picture of salvation. It's always on the move.

A REALISTIC ASSESSMENT: PROS AND CONS OF HOUSE CHURCHES

House churches have several things going for them:

- They are great for discipleship, fostering intimacy, and building community.
- Collaborative, grassroots house churches can help heal the wounds inflicted by hierarchical, authoritarian churches.
- They are often intergenerational, with children and youth taking important roles in worship.
- If they are started well, they are inherently evangelistic and welcoming.
- They may be attractive to folks who find large crowds and large buildings off-putting.
- They invite discussion and leadership development.
- With attention, they can become a networked system.
- They are cheap to start and run, since there are no buildings to maintain.

House churches have these potential drawbacks:

- It is hard to develop comprehensive Christian education for children and students.
- They are time- and energy-intensive for the pastor.
- They can be relationally messy, since they can attract strong personalities and emotionally needy or hurt people.
- If they are not started and nurtured well, they can become internally focused and cliquish.
- Some people may be uncomfortable about visiting a private residence, or they may prefer the anonymity of a larger church.
- Without attention, they can become isolated from a larger connection.
- Though they are cheap to start and run, they may have difficulty supporting professional staff.

Is House Church for Me?

If you are attracted to the idea of making disciples in an intimate setting, spreading good news among communities resistant to church, and changing the world by expanding the kin-dom, house churches might be a good fit for you. Of course, many legacy churches aim to do these things as well.

This is where a realistic assessment of the strengths and weaknesses of house church becomes important. The table on the previous page names some specific strengths and weaknesses of house churches. I'll address some of these in the "how-to" section of the book.

Embracing house churches as an effective way to be church and to meet the needs of individuals, the church, and society requires a shift in how we understand individuals and the communities of which they are a part. It requires a shift in the way we think of leadership and power, followership and decision-making. It may even require a shift in theology. The next chapter addresses the principles of organizing house churches to meet these needs.

CHAPTER 3

PRINCIPLES OF ORGANIZING HOUSE CHURCHES

A Farmer Scattered Seed

A farmer went out to scatter seed. As he was scattering seed, some fell on the path, and birds came and ate it. Other seed fell on rocky ground where the soil was shallow. They sprouted immediately because the soil wasn't deep. But when the sun came up, it scorched the plants, and they dried up because they had no roots. Other seed fell among thorny plants. The thorny plants grew and choked them. Other seed fell on good soil and bore fruit, in one case a yield of one hundred to one, in another case a yield of sixty to one, and in another case a yield of thirty to one. Everyone who has ears should pay attention.
—Matthew 13:3-9

After this parable and the one about this mustard shrub, I can imagine what the farmers in his audience would have said to him:

Stick to carpentry, Rabbi.[1]

If Jesus's listeners were perplexed by his substitution of mustard for cedar, this farmer would have confused them even more. Nobody farms this way! You don't waste seed by scattering it in a parking lot, across sidewalks, into bushes and drainage ditches. We know the right way to farm, and it's similar to what we teach church planters. You first do a soil analy-

---

1. Or masonry. *Tekton* means "builder," and most buildings in the area, even today, are made of stone, not wood.

sis: church planters are taught to carefully study their demographic maps, including data gathered by marketing professionals, in order to speak to the needs of particular people. Once your location is selected, you carefully dig a hole and plant your seed and nurture it until it becomes huge.

But planting house churches is more like what happens in the parable: you just plant them, flinging them into the world, recognizing that many of them will not last! Knowing that they both grow and die like weeds, recognizing the advantages of decentralized systems, and realizing how huge the growing population of people alienated from the institutional church is, we plant house churches willy-nilly. Just start something! God's extravagant grace means nothing is wasted in the long term. There will be a harvest.

While I don't dismiss the importance of cultural competence, knowing your mission field, and tailoring your message to a particular context, house church planting means applying that knowledge and those skills in different ways. While conventional church planting borrows principles from business entrepreneurship, for house churches, I prefer the language and principles of community organizing. What we're doing with house churches is not so much starting a business as *advancing a movement*.

There are some principles for house church planting in the parable that I've already mentioned in earlier chapters: focusing on the small (seeds), failing fast (scattering), and reproducing quickly (multiplication). The farmer also trusts in the chaordic, emergent system to develop its own organization and produce results. What the farmer is doing doesn't seem organized at all. It seems extremely disorganized! But a different kind of organizing emerges from his activity, and it's one we already have a name for: *grassroots*.

Perhaps the farmer trusts that God will give the growth. Perhaps the farmer trusts the seeds, the soil, and the emergent system to do its work. And perhaps these are just different words for the same thing.

Organizing to Beat the Devil

If John Wesley, the founder of Methodism, had a particular genius, it was not in his evangelistic preaching. By most accounts, he was not nearly the preacher that his friend George Whitfield was. Wesley's genius was in organizing. After bringing people to Christ or seeing them recommit to discipleship, he organized them into bands and classes that met during the week, each with a strong lay leader. Methodism was not a denomination at that point—it was a renewal movement among laypeople within the Church of England. And it spread like wildfire.

It's also relevant to our discussion of house churches to note that Francis Asbury, one of the first bishops of Methodism, lamented that as Methodists prospered financially, they grew more and more fixated on building large buildings. To him, this heralded a dangerous diversion from the original movement's emphasis on simplicity and ministry with the poor.[2]

Those original eighteenth-century groups continue to inspire small group discipleship movements in churches today. They had several characteristics that made them effective, and which they share with today's house churches. Some of these will sound familiar:

They were lay-led. It did not require a professional clergyperson to run a meeting.

They were simple. The Methodist societies had three simple rules: Do no harm, do good, and stay in love with God.[3]

They met in homes. They did not require dedicated space, and so were flexible. This made them especially effective in colonial North America where church buildings had not been built yet.

They emphasized mission. They expected people following Jesus—and not just clergy—to do certain concrete behaviors like visit prisons and hospitals, be good stewards of their resources, and act in loving and just ways in the local community. This was practical

---

2. "In May 1809, Asbury lamented that New England Methodists seemed intent on building 'grand' houses with steeples and pews, even if it meant stooping to hold lotteries to raise the money." From John H. Wigger, *American Saint: Francis Asbury and the Methodists* (New York: Oxford University Press, 2009), 367.

3. I am grateful for the way Bishop Rueben Job summarizes The General Rules of Methodist Societies in his *Three Simple Rules: A Wesleyan Way of Living* (Nashville: Abingdon Press, 2007).

discipleship. They had a sense that this mission was of cosmic and urgent importance.

They networked. Each society knew it was in relationship with other societies. Although each group knew its own community, a person could leave one meeting in one part of the country and drop into another in a different part of the country and expect a similar kind of accountability and focus.

They reproduced. Early Methodism was all about "spreading scriptural holiness throughout the land."[4] When Wesley trained preachers, he emphasized that getting new converts into new groups was absolutely essential. Conversion was pointless unless the new believer was incorporated into a community of support and sanctification.

Church leaders have been aware of these principles for ages, but it seems we are only beginning to appreciate this kind of grassroots, lay-led organizing in the last few decades. The idea of emergent systems and the emergent church has led to a new appreciation for decentralized, non-hierarchical forms of leadership. Part of Dee Hock's idea of "chaordic leadership"[5] is that most of our leading needs to be leading ourselves, and the next most important kind of leadership is leading up—telling people who lead us how we expect to be led and what we need to be effective. Leadership is not about managing underlings, but about taking responsibility for how we are led. One of my community organizer friends puts it this way: We are to be "architects of policy, not its subjects."

These grassroots, emergent systems have their own characteristics. Kester Brewin names several,[6] which I would argue are also part of a good house church strategy:

---

4. Wesley, "Minutes of Several Conversations between the Reverend Mr. John and Charles Wesley, and Others," in *Works*, 10:845, https://www.umcdiscipleship.org/blog/holiness-of-heart-and-life-conclusion-part-6-of-6#_ftn1.

5. Dee Hock, "The Art of Chaordic Leadership," *Leader to Leader Institute* (2000), http://www.griequity.com/resources/integraltech/GRIBusinessModel/chaordism/hock.html.

6. Kester Brewin, *Signs of Emergence: A Vision for Church That Is Organic, Networked, Decentralized, Bottom-up, Communal, Flexible, Always Evolving* (Grand Rapids: Baker, 2007).

Emergent systems are **open**, responding to their environment and accepting "cross-fertilization" from outside the system, instead of rejecting it all as "contamination."

They are **adaptable**, recognizing the need to change to fit their local environment.

They are **learning**, constantly analyzing how their parts are interrelated, opting for small-scale grassroots changes that may be outside of direct supervisory control. They recognize the importance of personal and institutional memory.

They **distribute knowledge**, meaning that there is no central "brain" that holds all the knowledge, but that knowledge and authority are rated and approved as trustworthy by the users. They are more like Wikipedia than like *Encyclopedia Britannica*.

They **model servant leadership**. Whereas conventional and institutional church has a number of big-name celebrity preachers, Brewin says churches that are truly emergent systems will be driven by many unknown leaders. In the words of some movement organizers, they are "leader-ful," not leaderless.

When we look at the church's grassroots past and compare it to our grassroots present, we can see the similarities: simplicity, openness, adaptability, reproducibility, networking, decentralization, and practical discipleship. These grassroots, emergent systems are not a new approach to leadership and organizing. They have always been around.

Organizing Communities Who Organize

When it comes to starting new churches, there is a field of knowledge the institutional church has often ignored or perhaps even avoided for several decades: the field of community organizing.

The term "community organizing" means what it says: gathering a community with a common interest and helping them organize to achieve changes in their community. Marshall Ganz defines community organizing as "leadership that enables people to turn the resources they have into the power they need to make the change they want."[7] Community organizers are people who want to be part of a movement that will change society. They train and develop leaders among a community who will work—and, if necessary, fight—for their rights.

Saul Alinsky's *Rules for Radicals*, which has become a sort of introductory and historical textbook for community organizers, was written in 1971.[8] But for many people, Barack Obama was the first name they heard associated with community organizing. For him, that meant organizing people in Chicago neighborhoods to demand better services from their elected officials. For labor organizers, it means gathering workers to demand better conditions. For migrant workers, it may mean gathering workers to fight against wage theft, sexual harassment, and other kinds of exploitation.

Because of its radical roots and anarchic approach to leadership, it's easy to see why some institutional-minded Christians might be wary of community organizing. Some conservative pundits use Saul Alinsky's name as a curse word.[9] But faith-based community organizing has a long history. The Quakers were instrumental in abolishing the slave trade in England and advancing the abolitionist movement in the United States, and it was in part their "starfish" nature, their decentralized, nonhierarchical, faith-based organizing that helped them do it.[10] Harriet Tubman in the Underground Railroad, Dorothy Day in the Catholic Worker Movement, Martin Luther King Jr. in the civil rights movement, and Dietrich

---

7. Marshall Ganz, *Organizing: People, Power, Change* (Leading Change Network, 2014), https://d3n8a8pro7vhmx.cloudfront.net/themes/52e6e37401925b6f9f000002/attachments/original/1423171411/Organizers_Handbook.pdf?1423171411.

8. Saul David Alinsky, *Rules for Radicals: A Practical Primer for Realistic Radicals*, 1st ed. (New York: Random House, 1971).

9. In 2016, Ben Carson implied that Hillary Clinton was evil, since she wrote about Alinsky, and Alinsky's book includes a reference to "the very first radical" who "won his own kingdom," Lucifer. Anyone who has worked for change against the status quo gets used to being called a devil, including Jesus: "It's enough for disciples to be like their teacher and slaves like their master. If they have called the head of the house Beelzebul, it's certain that they will call the members of his household by even worse names" (Matthew 10:25). More than one Christian has told me I'm going to hell, so I consider myself in good company.

10. Brafman and Beckstrom, *The Starfish and the Spider*, 98.

Bonhoeffer in the Confessing Church movement are all examples of well-known faith-based organizers. There is good reason for institutions who value stability and the status quo to fear such people! I believe many people who have left the institutional church long to be part of such movements.

For a multiracial faith-based community organizing group I'm affiliated with, community organizing means pressuring city officials to reduce homicides in Birmingham. Instead of simply demanding more policing and surveillance, which only responds after violence, we advocate a different solution: investing in street outreach workers and proven anti-violence strategies before a crime happens.

Community organizing, like early Methodism, is "organizing to beat the devil," and it is similarly often carried out among populations that many respectable middle- and upper-class Christians avoid: poor neighborhoods, citizens returning from prison, undocumented immigrants, or sex workers. Instead of viewing these populations as passive subjects to be saved by church people, they are the ones whose voices matter, whose stories are centered, who lead and strategize. One of the main principles of grassroots community organizing is that those closest to the pain of injustice are the best equipped and most knowledgeable about the solutions they need. Far too often, government agencies, churches, and other do-gooders think they know what is needed to solve homelessness, and yet they have no homeless or formerly homeless people in leadership of their organizations. Grassroots leadership means supporting leaders who actually represent the roots.

Community organizers believe that it is just as important to talk about power as it is to talk about love. Power is the ability to create change, to influence one's environment. This may mean creating and advocating for a policy or toppling a dictatorship.

It also means that we must be aware of how power operates between individuals at the group level. Who gets to speak? When? Whose ideas have more weight? Does this power depend on the age, race, sex, gender identity, sexual orientation, religion, or physical or mental ability of the speaker? And what would Jesus say about that? Power, then, is not just an abstract thing we talk about externally; it's something we recognize and must be honest about internally. If I'm a white, straight preacher in a house church of people who are mostly black and gay—which happens once a week—I need to be aware of the power dynamics in the room and outside of it. If I'm in a house church made up mostly of women who are nurses, I similarly need to recognize where the limits of my knowledge are, and who gets to speak, for example, about the woman with the issue of blood who touched the hem of Jesus's robe (Luke 8:43-48). The act of teaching and proclamation itself must become part of the discussion about power (see chapter 10).

Organizers often use the language of faith, speaking of prophetic imagination, spiritual warfare, and resisting powers and principalities. They also emphasize decentralized, grassroots leadership, network with one another, and encourage their groups to reproduce. Black Lives Matter is a great example of a grassroots mass movement that is simple, nonhierarchical, and grassroots. When media pundits and thought leaders have complained that there is no "leader" to the movement, members respond, "We are not leader-less; we are leader-full."[11]

This decentralized, leader-full network is exactly the way the early church spread. Walter Wink said, "Killing Jesus was like trying to destroy a dandelion seed-head by blowing on it. It was like shattering the sun into a million fragments of light."[12] Even when Rome was trying its hardest to destroy the church by persecuting its members and killing its leaders, it succeeded only in scattering and spreading the seeds further and further. Simple, decentralized, lay-led organizations are almost impossible to kill.

Community organizers repeat some common lessons that house church planters should take to heart:

Identify your self-interest: This is fundamental to community organizing. As a Christian raised in churches, I'd always been taught that we should be altruistic and put others' needs above our own. It may seem shocking to prioritize our self-interest. But generations of paternalism, failed missionary charities, and "meddling" social programs that do more

---

11. Danielle C. Belton, "Leaderless or Leader-ful?" *The Root* (August 10, 2015), https://www.theroot.com/leaderless-or-leader-ful-1790860733.

12. Walter Wink, *Engaging the Powers: Discernment and Resistance in a World of Domination*, The Powers (Minneapolis: Fortress, 1992), 154.

harm than good have taught us the danger of dishonest altruism. Charlene Carruthers, one of the cofounders of the Black Lives Matter movement, puts it this way:

> Selflessness is problematic because it is devoid of someone's vision for the world and their place in it. Self-interest, on the other hand, situates you, your vision, and your values in relationship with others. Identifying self-interest is essential because it allows individuals to work not simply as allies but as accomplices in our collective liberation.[13]

If I am hurting and you want me to trust you, I need to understand that you are not serving out of altruism, but out of common self-interest: You have my back. There is no hierarchy or shame in identifying and naming your self-interest.[14]

Ask, "Who are my people?": Experienced church planters have long observed that leaders do better in their own "affinity group." This does not mean we should stay in our own segregated bubbles—rural, working-class folks with rural, working-class folks; white folks with white folks; and so on—but that in organizing a community, we have to recognize our own. Any mission that is generically "for everybody" is truly for nobody and destined for failure. House churches will thrive best if there is some kind of affinity, even if it is just geographical location.

In addition to helping people come to a greater self-understanding, house churches that help people identify "their people" also help them reach beyond family and tribe. The existential question for many of us is not just "Who am I?" but "Who am I in relation to who *we* are? How can I be authentically myself in a community of similarity and difference?" House churches can help each person understand their selfhood and their story in relation to the community and to the movement of what God is doing in the world.

---

13. Charlene A. Carruthers, *Unapologetic: A Black, Queer, and Feminist Mandate for Our Movement* (Boston: Beacon, 2018), 67.

14. For a great introduction to faith-based community organizing that recommends Christian solidarity instead of the Alinsky-style focus on self-interest, see Alexia Salvatierra, *Faith-Rooted Organizing: Mobilizing the Church in Service to the World* (Downers Grove, IL: InterVarsity, 2014).

Share personal stories: We do this in groups, in one-to-one meetings, and in calling people to action. For example, an organizer might tell a story about how their grandfather died from black lung disease working in coal mines, and how her family suffered when the mine failed to help them. This is why she is passionate about working in poor neighborhoods in the shadow of a coal-fired power plant where rates of childhood asthma and cancer are three times higher than average. One of the leaders she recruits is a mother who tells the group about her nine-year-old's respiratory illness, and how many times they've been to the hospital, and how much money it costs her. These stories help the group identify their self-interest, build relationships, and move toward action.

In house churches, the role of stories is similar. Sermons give way to discussion which gives way to testimony. People share stories of their past and how it shapes their outlook now. These are moments of bonding and growth for the group, and often inform what we do next. For example, a number of our members have shared memories of what being in nature has meant to them, as well as their grief over climate change. That led us to focus on creation care for Lent and led to a community tree-planting service. This was not something that I came up with as a program for the group, but an idea that emerged and developed over the course of a year through the stories we told.

Build relationships: The most versatile tool in the organizer's tool belt is one-to-one conversations. In church terms, one-to-ones are evangelism, discipleship, recruitment, accountability, identifying ministry opportunities, and many other core activities of church. I believe it is not a coincidence that Jesus pointed out that he was present "wherever two or more are gathered." Relationships are also important in the rest of organizing work: in creating a sense of community and in building relationships with elected officials or people in power.

Develop leadership: "Organizers teach and leaders organize" is another common saying. The best organizers are not simply rallying people to carry signs. They are doing leadership development. They are coaches who help identify and grow community leaders. If an organizer is doing most of the work—making sure there are refreshments at the meeting, signing people in and making sure they have name tags, doing most of the speaking at the meeting—they are making the same mistake as an overfunctioning pastor. Good organizers and good pastors get other people to lead.

Create simple structure: "Structures channel power" is one of the slogans of community organizing. A group cannot simply come together and complain. Like any living organism, they need at least a rudimentary structure. A structure does not need to be bureaucratic and overly complicated, but it is important to know who is responsible for what piece of the work. Again, in creating structure, it is important to remember to center the voices of the people who are most affected.

This is something we are always struggling with and revising. Our network has a simple "leadership team" made up of representatives from each house church, plus some leaders who fulfill certain roles (treasurer, secretary, official lay spokesperson). Each house church has a host family and core group who are the leaders.

Strategize: Community organizers encourage their leaders to do "research actions," to meet with experts and officials to learn all they can about the problem. In the example of pollution, they might meet with medical professionals to learn about health problems, with scientists to learn about environmental issues, with activists and sociologists to learn about environmental racism, with corporate officials to learn about policy, and with elected officials to learn about who they need to influence. The slogan here is "go in dumb, come out smart." They start with a general problem (like "pollution," for example) and then figure out how to address a particular policy issue (like laws about the regulation of particulate matter). By the time they meet with corporate executives and elected people in power, they won't allow those in power to talk down to them, to distract, delay, or deny. They name names and identify who they need to talk to and what specific demands they want to make.

Take concrete action: The time line from telling stories about asthma to getting a specific policy change might take years, and it will probably require many individual and group actions. But eventually there is a measurable outcome. There is something for a group to celebrate.

While it's important to note that house church planting is not the same as community organizing—churches are about more than changing policy and empowering communities—many of the principles are the same. This is because both are rooted in the notion that systemic change happens by forming people in community to use their God-given power—whether that power is political, social, or spiritual.

Working the House Church Ecosystem

I've chosen to use the language and principles of community organizing to talk about how we do house churches, but I'm aware that there are other models and other ways to talk about it. Some church planters I know prefer to root everything they do in the language of the Bible, to emphasize the idea that their church really is like the early church. Some church planters use the language of social or business entrepreneurship.

This brings me to where house churches fit in the church "ecosystem." I see at least five different groups of people who have something to contribute to the discussion of house churches, each with their own languages, perspectives, goals, and values. Sometimes these groups cooperate and communicate with one another, and sometimes they regard one another with suspicion or even antipathy.

The illustration on the following page is a graphic representation of how I think of house churches cooperating with the institutional and non-institutional church. Groups at the top are ones we associate more with the institutional church, and groups at the bottom are the ones that tend to be more organic and grassroots in nature. Most church folks who are comfortable with institutional forms of organization feel at home among the top three. Non-church folks and nonconformist Christians tend to gravitate toward the bottom. "Spiritual but not religious" folks will definitely be toward the bottom as well.

This is not a Venn diagram. In real life, the boundaries are fuzzy, and people may inhabit more than one group. But each group tends to have its own language and mental models for how they approach the world.

Chapter 3

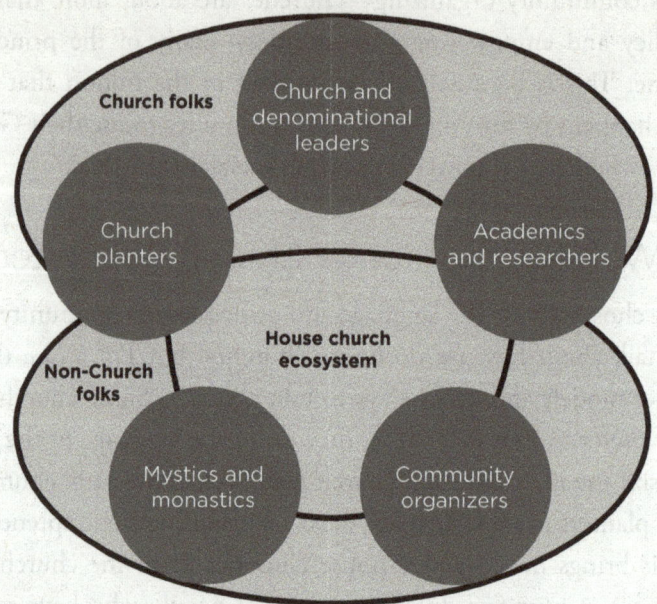

Church Planters

The first group uses the language of church planters, some of whom may be house church enthusiasts, and some of whom aim to start megachurches. They tend to be evangelical and speak about a new thing the Holy Spirit is doing that has roots in the early church and exciting possibilities for the future. Though they are not universally so, they tend to lean conservative, either theologically, politically, or both. By and large, even if they regard the institutional church as a dinosaur, they talk easily with denominational leaders from institutional churches, because they have a shared religious language and a goal of seeing the gospel spread. They use phrases like "seeking guidance from the Lord," "bathing the process in prayer," and finding wise "people of peace" who will "speak into your life." They may also talk with folks from less institutional and more radical forms of community, folks I call "mystics and monastics."

Denominational Leaders

The second group uses the language of denominations and judicatories, and leaders of institutional churches. This group sees house churches as one of a number of possible "fresh expressions" of church life. These are folks who are aware of the multiple crises facing the church of the next years and decades, and they want to encourage church planting both for the spread of the gospel and for the survival of the institution. They use phrases like "social entrepreneurship" and "innovative, healthy, effective ministry." Though they may be circumspect about equating success with faithfulness and numerical growth with health, they are dealing with the material conditions of the future of the institution: You can't do ministry without bodies and bucks. They talk easily with church planters, whom they regard as their gifted but slightly wild cousins doing important work. They also talk with sociologists, theologians, and other academics who study the church and larger culture.

Academics

This third group uses the language of academic theology and sociology. They also study house churches as one possible answer to many complex social and historical pressures. Luther Smith, for example, recognizes house churches as one form of intentional community and has studied a number of alternatives to institutional church. Sociologists like Robert Wuthnow look at demographic trends and describe how the economy has changed the family, which in turn has changed the church, and what that means for the future. Leonard Sweet and George Barna are other folks who do statistical research into the sociology of church life. Their language is generally more descriptive than prescriptive, but they talk about demographics, statistics, and cultural trends that affect the church. This academic group talks easily with denominational leaders, who want to learn from them. They are also the most natural communicators with faith-based community organizers.

Chapter 3

Faith-Based Community Organizers

The fourth group uses the language of faith-based community organizing. Though they are doing similar (and sometimes identical) work to the group of church planters, they tend to lean more liberal than conservative. Sometimes they defy easy political and theological pigeonholing: some of the most Marxist Christians I know take the Bible very literally! Though they may be people of faith and even do community organizing through a faith lens, the lines of communication between them and the church planters and denominational leaders are often strained. People who do community organizing talk most freely about disruption, of upending hierarchies. They are all about the power of God working through people, but may sometimes feel that the coming Kingdom depends all upon them and their effort. They must have deep wells of spiritual nourishment or else they burn out. They often share language with academics, who talk freely about class, race, and power. They also share much in common with the mystics and monastics.

Mystics and Monastics

This fifth group is radically experimental in how they conceive of social life and the gospel. They may live in intentional communities in co-housing or co-living arrangements. Sometimes they take vows of poverty and share property in common. They often deliberately choose a different lifestyle from North American capitalism. Sometimes they start businesses with a strong ministry component. One such business in my town fixes up old bicycles and sells them, but also gives bikes to homeless people who need transportation. Another café often lets religious groups use its space for free. These people tend to be all over the place theologically and politically. They may or may not attend a legacy church, because their tight community is their church. This group is often the most natural connection between community organizers and church planters, who often approach the world and their faith from very different angles.

Do you see yourself in one or more of these groups? When we talk about "the Church" with a capital *C*, I believe it includes all of them. And it bears repeating that the boundaries are fluid. Mystics and monastics give workshops at megachurches, CEO-preachers go on silent retreats in intentional communities, academics preach from pulpits, and prophetic activists who are working for the Kingdom are in boardrooms and ivory towers as well as in the streets.

These groups have their own languages and interests, but they share a passion for Jesus's world-changing and life-transforming good news. But I think it's important to name these groups and their interests, because house churches can have dialogue with and learn from all of them. I have spent time in each of these communities both as a recipient and contributor of direction and wisdom. Understanding where house churches fit into an ecosystemic relation to the other groups can help us avoid binary distinctions between "house churches" and "the institutional church."

I recommend that anyone starting a house church look for wisdom from more than one of these sources. All of them have possible resources for house church leaders and opportunities for partnerships. This is the "open" principle of emergent systems that welcomes and invites cross-pollination and distributed knowledge. This kind of sampling will assist house churches to develop the DNA necessary to survive as decentralized, nonhierarchical, self-replicating systems.

Summary

Before we get to the "how-to" portion of this book, I'd like to recap some of the principles I've mentioned so far. Effective house churches:

Grow from the **grassroots**: Leadership is not hierarchical. We lead horizontally and we lead up.

Follow the principle of **mustard weed growth**: Stay focused on reproduction and tenacity, not growing large. "Fail fast."

Have **simple systems**: Simplicity means ideas are easier to remember and replicate.

Focus on **practical discipleship**: We are about practices, not programs.

Acknowledge we are **co-learners**: We learn and distribute knowledge; we teach and shape one another.

Stay **open and adaptable**: Receive wisdom from anywhere, including legacy churches.

Understand how house church fits into the **larger ecosystem**.

Tell stories and **build relationships**: Time spent in one-to-one conversation and group discussion is never wasted. It all builds community.

Grow **self-understanding**: Help folks identify their self-interest and "their people." Help them discover how to be authentically themselves within a group that welcomes their authenticity.

PART TWO
HOW DO WE START A HOUSE CHURCH?

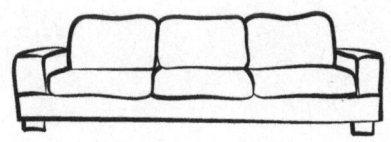

PART TWO

HOW DO WE START A HOUSE CHURCH?

CHAPTER 4
ASSEMBLING THE FIRST GROUP

Assembling the Group

It will start with a conversation between you and one other person, or a couple of friends. They may feel nudged to try something different. They may feel like churches they've visited are all looking for a transactional relationship with them, instead of a transformational one. You ask, half-joking, "Why don't we start a church?" They don't laugh.

Maybe you've already had that conversation and you're farther down the road. You may understand that you and your friend are already a "church," because of the "where two or more are gathered" principle. But there's someone else they know who would be interested in this, and church isn't church if it doesn't spread good news. So now you are more.

At some point, you will likely have heady discussion about *what church is and is not*. These are great discussions and you should come back to them again and again. You will probably share stories of highs and lows in churches you've attended before, and you may agree or disagree about what "the primary purpose of church" is.

Worship

But if I'm in your group, here's the place I do not budge: the main activity of a house church is worship.

45

Worship distinguishes a house church from a Bible study or a "small group," which may be a program of a larger church. This is not a class meeting, or a Sunday school class, or a Bible study, though it may share elements of all of those, and all of those may share elements of worship. But we know and identify a church because it is a group of people who come together to worship. That may look like studying the Bible, and it may look like service, and it may or may not include singing and preaching or testimony, but if the participants don't understand it as worship, then they don't understand themselves as a church. If we gather and eat a common meal, read scripture, sing a few songs, and leave, that's fine—as long as everyone understands that what we've just done is worship and gives glory to God. If we do nothing but sit in meditative silence and breathe, that's fine—as long as everyone understands that what we're doing is worship as a church.

There are several reasons it's important for people to understand what they are doing as worship. First, worship is important for establishing the group identity as a "real church." House church members are not "playing church," and participation is not simply an extracurricular activity.

Second, if the core group signs up expecting that they'll one day "graduate" to a building with a "real" worship service (unless that is your intention), they may be disappointed. While I always leave open the possibility that the Holy Spirit could lead a particular house church into a different expression of church someday, I try to make it clear that becoming an attractional, event-focused church is not the main agenda.

Finally, worship is the place we make holy time and holy space to encounter God. We may or may not have a discernible encounter with God during worship, but as a community we create the space to do so. We may encounter God privately during the week, of course, in any number of ways, and bring news of this encounter back to the community during public worship. But this public act of our community making space for God, and God making space for us, is what takes our discipleship beyond mere human programs of self-improvement.

If your philosophy of ministry is different, that's fine. But your core group needs to be on the same page about why you exist as a church! "We come together to ____" is the first thing your core group must agree on.

Teaching and Learning

The first step in turning the core group into a functional house church is helping one another understand what a house church is and isn't, and what your mission is. Your core group needs to be folks who buy into the vision of creating a network of organically reproducing house churches. This is not a mutual-admiration society for people who are too enlightened or spiritually advanced for legacy churches. They do not need to be folks who merely have an ax to grind with "the institutional church" (although some ax-grinding is probably fine and normal; I'll share more on ax-grinding and group dynamics in a later chapter).

Learning the principles of house churches is the first thing the core group needs to do. There is plenty to discuss, and plenty of personal experiences to share, among just a handful of people. You may come up with other principles or nonnegotiables in your group that I've missed.

There are a few hard lessons I've had to learn about starting house churches. There are three rules that I try to follow when starting a house church:

1. A house church requires a core group of three households. A "household" can be a single person or a family, but three is the minimum number who will make a commitment to be there nearly every week. This way, if someone is sick or out of town, we can still have church, because wherever two or more are gathered, Jesus is there.
2. The three households do a trial run for four to six weeks, during which they figure out stuff like childcare, structure, and what will work for them. This trial period is important because it establishes the practices that will be passed on to future generations of house churches.

3. At the end of the trial run, they commit to join as members (in our churches, we call them "partners") and to meet consistently for eight months. We've tried starting house churches with people who are not partners, or who were members of another church but who volunteered their home, and it simply hasn't worked long-term for us. For the core group, this needs to be *their* church, not an extracurricular activity.

Simple and Flexible

Among the core group, it's important to establish *keeping it simple* as a general principle. We use a simple liturgy available in book form or online,[1] we pray, read scripture, and share a message with discussion. We conclude with communion, then share business and announcements at the end. We do not pass an offering plate, as that feels awkward in a small group and nearly all of our giving is done online. Everything we do is designed to be easily replicable. If I, the pastor, am not available, the members need to be able to carry on without me.

I also emphasize to the group that this is their church, meaning our schedule, how we structure worship, and any local traditions we develop are up to them. For example, one of our house churches is not big on singing, so we sing rarely if at all. But for another, singing is an important part of their worship experience, so we sing every time we gather. In one church, in order to include children in more aspects of worship, they process parts of the table setting into the room: a table runner, flowers, a candle (battery-powered—we've learned from experience that open flame is a bad idea), chalice, and paten.

Hosting

The idea of hosting a weekly gathering sometimes makes people nervous. It's one thing to talk inspirationally about "radical hospitality," but

---

1. Shane Claiborne, Jonathan Wilson-Hartgrove, and Enuma Okoro, *Common Prayer: A Liturgy for Ordinary Radicals* (Grand Rapids: Zondervan, 2010); see also http://common prayer.net.

it's another to ask potential strangers into your home week after week. This is one of many reasons it's important that core families have an alternative location, both to give hosts a break and to have an option for when folks are sick or on vacation.

The first few meetings are about setting precedent. A host does not need to create a space that looks like the feature of a home design magazine or lay out a spread that looks like it belongs on a foodie blog. This kind of over-performing makes it less likely anyone else will want to host. While providing snacks, coffee, or other signs of hospitality makes community more intimate—and we want the space to be comfortable—we prefer what Rev. Jack King calls "scruffy hospitality,"[2] so that people without the resources, fancy furniture, or privilege of wealth feel comfortable hosting. A little dog hair on the couch is okay, as long as we're sure nobody's allergies will suffer too much. We frequently serve biscuits and jam at our morning gathering at our house, along with a vegan alternative. This is more than enough for most gatherings.

That is, of course, unless your group wants to make preparing and eating dinner part of their ritual!

Another important thing I tell hosts is that house church is not meant to be a burden on one household. If meeting weekly becomes stressful, I'd rather people not host, or take a break, than to keep going until they resent the community and burn out. What I find, though, is that hosts usually come to enjoy cleaning up and preparing for guests once a week. It certainly helps us keep our house tidier, and some hosts tell me it feels like a luxury to not scramble to get loaded into the car every week. When church comes to you, it can reduce stress instead of increasing it.

This is also why the trial run is important. Hosts get to try out how hosting a house church will fit into their lifestyle, and we get to see what will work and what will not work in a new location. We get a chance to see what the personality of the new house church will be.

---

2. Jack King, "Why Scruffy Hospitality Creates Space for Friendship." *KnoxPriest.com* (May 21, 2014). The original link is missing, but it is archived here: https://web.archive.org/web/20140614085151/; http://www.knoxpriest.com/scruffy-hospitality-creates-space-friendship/.

Chapter 4

I also tell the core group that if it doesn't work out, it's okay. In the parable of the sower, the farmer casts seed far and wide, and not every seed will take. While we'd love for every single house church to germinate and flourish in fertile soil, we have to be willing to fail and call it quits. Making lots of mistakes is how we've succeeded so far.

Once you've assembled your core group, made sure everyone is on the same page, and established expectations for the host and your trial run, you are ready for your first worship gathering.

CHAPTER 5
WORSHIP IN HOUSE CHURCHES

Let us use this new word, Churchbeing, *because words like* community *and* church *are misused, overused, abused, and confused. Churches think they're a community because that is what the word* church *suggests, without realizing how much the technological milieu hinders us from really caring for each other with the gutsy, sacrificial love of genuine community.*

—Marva Dawn[1]

Church leaders often make the distinction between "going to church" and "being the church." We make a similar distinction between "attractional" and "missional" churches.[2] Worship is not simply an event we attend where we watch professionals say inspirational things and play impressive music. We can get that by queuing up TED Talks and listening to inspirational music on our streaming platform of choice.

True, we can "worship" on our own, if by worship we mean direct our attention to God, pray, or seek spiritual experience. Most of us have encountered someone—or we *are* someone—who says they experience God better in nature than in a pew. We can read the Bible, meditate, practice yoga, pray, dance, make love, fly a kite, or eat magic mushrooms—all of

---

1. Marva J. Dawn, *A Royal Waste of Time: The Splendor of Worshiping God and Being Church for the World* (Grand Rapids: Eerdmans, 1999), 121.

2. See Alan Hirsch, *The Forgotten Ways: Reactivating the Missional Church* (Grand Rapids: Brazos, 2006). See also Reggie McNeal, *Missional Renaissance: Changing the Scorecard for the Church*, 1st ed. (San Francisco: Jossey-Bass, 2009).

these can be powerful, life-altering spiritual experiences in which we encounter God.

But worship is more than practicing a discipline or chasing a spiritual experience. I believe a better term for this kind of individual activity is *devotion* (which I will discuss more in the next chapter). *Corporate worship* is central to Christian practice. There is something important, theologically, about being in the company of others while we give God praise. Corporate worship reminds us simultaneously of our vertical connection to God and our horizontal connection to our neighbors. Hearing multiple voices unite as one in singing, chanting, or praying gives us a different insight into our creatureliness before our Creator: I am one among many, yet we are all one in Christ.

This naturally leads to the question, "Well, if being part of a crowd is good, isn't a larger crowd better?"

Sometimes, absolutely. Some of my best experiences as an associate pastor at a large church were sitting in the chancel, with the pipe organ on my left and the congregation on my right, with the choir in front of me and an orchestra behind. I had the best seat in the house. All the audiophile engineers on the planet could not deliver that kind of sound with the best theater sound systems or expensive headphones. People who could sit in that space without the top of their heads coming off and their spirits leaping into the rafters would have to be made of stone. I wish everyone could have that kind of experience regularly.

This brings us back to the tension between the attractional and missional forms of worship. As a church planter going to workshops on worship, I've often been told that what worship planners at attractional churches should try to do is give people a "God moment," a spiritual experience of transcendence that puts our lives in perspective. While I believe such experiences are vital to our spiritual growth and that we can increase their predictable frequency, the other part of worship is spiritual training, reorientation, and connecting our transcendental experience with the practical everyday business of living in the world. We should leave worship ready to be in mission to the world. Coming before God in worship should be neither a grim duty we undertake to "build character," nor a chasing of a spiritual high. I believe it is the community itself that grounds us in reality, in our humanity, and in Christ's divinity.

While it is not only possible but important to worship with strangers, the word *community* requires a context. These are real live people with whom we sing, share communion, and read the Bible. Without ongoing relationships that allow us to be authentically ourselves among a community that has both intimacy and mission, as Luther Smith says, we miss some of the transformational power that worship has.

House churches allow us to worship in a context where our neighbors know our struggles, our hopes, and our history. When we bring our own experience to worship and ask for prayer or offer our unique perspective on a scripture during discussion, we're letting the Holy Spirit into our lives to do spiritual work. When we let our defenses down and become vulnerable with people who actually know us, we can experience God in an intimate way.

It is not uncommon, for example, to have people in a house church share with the group how a scripture challenges them, or to weep when telling about their hard week and how God has felt distant to them, or to laugh out loud when they make a personal connection to wisdom from Proverbs and a situation at work. Though we may not have pipe organs and choirs, and though the awe we feel may be a quieter kind, the spiritual experience and the practical lessons are no less powerful.

Why Do We Worship?

"Why do we worship?" is not what people ask. They ask, "How do you worship in a house church?" They might mean, "How do you structure your worship time together?" Sometimes I can see the look of apprehension on someone's face when they ask, and I can tell that they are thinking of worship in terms of three songs and a sermon. They are thinking, correctly, that this would be painfully awkward among a dozen people in a house church.

But the implicit question, the question they do not ask, is about why, and related to it is the question, *what constitutes worship*? This question shapes how we form this new house church community. With a new

Chapter 5

group, I find it helpful to (1) frame worship as a natural human behavior, (2) teach folks about the breadth and diversity of worship expression in Christian history, and (3) recognize people's spiritual longings and felt needs regarding worship.

If you've already got strong opinions about what "proper" worship is, I'm going to ask you to suspend your judgment for a moment. Let's not over-theologize this question. Yes, worship means giving glory to God, and our worship is due God. But if we are forming a community in the image of God, we need to begin with the human beings *in which God's image already resides*. Human beings have a built-in need to worship and have been doing it in many different ways for tens of thousands of years. It is a natural human behavior. God implanted in us a desire to worship, so we need to take this human desire seriously, especially if we're asking people raised in legacy churches to give up something familiar and try something new that they may not even recognize as "worship."

I take a very, very long view of worship. Creation itself is an act of worship simply by being itself. Psalm 19 (NIV) begins, "The heavens declare the glory of God." The Talmud says that each blade of grass has an angel bent over it whispering, "Grow! Grow!" Fyodor Dostoevsky wrote that "every blade of grass, every little insect, ant, every little golden bee," is worshiping, "for the Word is for all, all creation and all creatures, every little leaf is striving towards the Word, sings glory to God."[3] Humans, as part of creation and as social animals, are built to worship in community.

The oldest archaeological site in the world is in Turkey, at Gobekli Tepe, which was built about 11,000 years ago.[4] Not only do these giant stone rings predate the most ancient writings of the Bible by a good eight thousand years, their discovery has also rewritten the dominant theories of religion and civilization. It once was thought that humans developed agriculture before they developed complex social structure and religious life, but it turns out that worship predated agriculture, towns, and domesti-

---

3. F. Dostoevsky, R. Pevear, and L. Volokhonsky, *The Brothers Karamazov: A Novel in Four Parts with Epilogue* (New York: Farrar, Straus and Giroux, 2002), 295.

4. Andrew Curry, "Gobekli Tepe: The World's First Temple?" *Smithsonian Magazine* (November 2008), https://www.smithsonianmag.com/history/gobekli-tepe-the-worlds-first-temple-83613665/.

cated animals by thousands of years. We were worshiping together before we were farming! We built sacred spaces before we built cities.

When we move the clock forward a few thousand years, we see another trend that should inform the way we think about religion today. Sports are also a form of worship: the Olympics among the Greeks and games like tlatchtli and jai alai among the Maya are examples of sports that were part of their religion and culture. People competed to bring glory to the gods. Today, sports are still full of ritual, including chanting, singing the national anthem or team songs, and sacred animals (although we call them mascots). If you don't believe these rituals and symbols are sacred, just try sitting in your seat and talking during the national anthem, or intentionally messing up the wave, and observe how people around you react! When pastors complain that Sunday is no longer sacred because families attend sporting events, they are mistaken. Sundays are still sacred. It's just that church is competing with a different religion!

When I start a house church, this anthropological perspective of worship is one of the first things I try to teach the new group. I cast the net wide around these forms of worship because I think it's important for people leading house churches to understand how human beings worship across time and cultures. Worship through the centuries has been a way that we come together as a community and give glory to the Divine because it meets a fundamental, God-given human need. When we think about worship in homes or small settings, whether it is around a dining table or in a living room or on a front porch, we connect it with human activity that goes back before history was written down. I believe helping people see this historical perspective allows them to suspend some of their expectations, to wipe the slate clean, and consider the worship practices they think are most important and why.

I also think it's important to cast a wide net because some house church enthusiasts use a lot of "ought" and "should" language about worship, and a passionate few have chosen the house church model in order to enforce their particular view. While there are certainly biblical examples for what makes "proper" worship, I am highly skeptical of our tendency to come up with theological justifications for our preferences and prejudices. There is a tremendous diversity of worship practices among Christian traditions, from Palestinian Christians in Bethlehem to African American Christians in Chicago. In my opinion, house churches are a great opportunity for adventurous disciples to try out a number of practices that we might be reluctant to try in larger gatherings.

For people who are used to worship in a legacy church, house church worship provides an opportunity to do some healthy self-reflection and exploration about how worship affects us spiritually. It's pretty clear that there are some things that are not going to fly in house churches: guitar solos, liturgical dance, big-screen videos, or mass choirs, to name a few. For many people, these creative expressions are the things that define dynamic worship. They may have nostalgic memories or strong cultural preferences about what constitutes worship and will need to be invited to frame it in broader terms. And no matter how charismatic or exceptional a preacher might be, delivering a conversational message to a dozen people sitting in a circle in a living room is not the same as preaching from a pulpit to a crowd of thousands.

There is always some aspect of *performance* and *drama* to worship, no matter how large or small. But in our North American context, where size is seen as an indicator of success, we often perceive a performance that draws a large number of people as more *successful*. This is not an accident. Attractional churches have to compete with many other demands on people's attention and schedules: children's sports or other after-school activities, jobs, vacations, mass media, and mobile device screens, just to name a few. A legacy church with the attractional power to get people to come to worship has succeeded in cutting through the noise of distraction in a powerful way.

Of course, house church leaders may want to invite members to shift their criteria for evaluating worship from *successful* to *faithful*. But I think it is unwise for house church leaders to miss the importance of performance and drama to people's spiritual lives, so think strategically about how to partner with legacy churches to meet this legitimate human need. Members with strong musical backgrounds are going to miss the soaring melodies and celebratory sound of a good gospel or classical choir.

Some of our house churches take occasional "field trips" to friendly legacy churches to meet this need. We partner with other small churches for worship around high holy days like Christmas and Easter. This is part of recognizing the role that house churches play in the church ecosystem. There are some things house churches just can't do as well alone as we can do together.

How Do We Worship?

Should we structure our time together, or let the Holy Spirit lead things spontaneously? I've heard this binary question since I was young, phrased in different ways about different things: Should we use prewritten prayers or speak from the heart? Prepare sermons or extemporize?

I do not believe there is one right way to do public worship. My preference is to have a mix of scripted and spontaneous worship. My charismatic siblings may be more comfortable following the leading of the Holy Spirit in the moment, but I believe the Holy Spirit can speak during preparation as well. House churches are a great place to experiment with different approaches.

In the house church literature, some authors say that house churches should have no formal order or liturgy, and resist any attempt to create one. It is the Spirit who should guide worship, they say. Songs and prayers should be spontaneous. Part of the resistance to a formal order of worship is explicitly a reaction to the professionalization of worship in legacy churches. One author of a house church book quotes Paul saying, "When you come together, everyone has a hymn, a word of instruction, a revelation, a tongue, or an interpretation." And then asks, "Had scripture used the words 'only one' instead of 'everyone,' which would be more descriptive of most modern church services? . . . In a sense, there wasn't any audience because all of the brothers [sic] were potential cast members."[5]

I should note that Quakers have been worshiping in this egalitarian way since the 1600s, though their manifestation of the inspiration of the Holy Spirit tends to be focused more on listening than speaking. Tom

---

5. "Participatory Meetings," in *House Church,* ed. Steve Atkerson (Atlanta: New Testament Reformation Fellowship, 2008), 50.

Stave, a presiding elder of the Northwest Yearly Meeting of Friends, refers to this democratic kind of worship as "potluck worship."[6] There is certainly some overlap, both in leadership philosophy and in worship, in the way Spirit-led house churches operate and the form of worship advocated by the Society of Friends.

I advise our house churches to structure part of their time together with a devotional book or simple liturgy. I use a pre-written devotional or worship guide for three main reasons.

First, a devotional or worship guide gives nonprofessionals the confidence to lead. Not everyone feels comfortable extemporizing on the spot. On measures of fear, people consistently rank public speaking higher than death. And in some ways, speaking to a small group can be more intimidating than speaking to a stadium of thousands. While I do believe conquering our fears, especially of speaking publicly, is a sign of spiritual growth, I think a wise leader will recognize people need some training.

Second, extemporaneous prayers and sermons often begin to sound alike. The truth is, we rely on stock metaphors, phrases, and rhetorical commonplaces when we speak. When the pressure is on and we are speaking in front of a group, we tend to rely on our old favorite standbys even more. Our extemporized prayers and "spontaneous" worship can become repetitive. We develop a rote liturgy even when we do not mean to. This doesn't mean worship is not powerful or meaningful to participants, but it does become limiting. It's always good advice for people who want to be authors to read a lot. In a similar way, we can teach people to pray by having them read other prayers. It opens up new ways to address God and gives us language that allows us to express ourselves even better.

Third, if groups tend to naturally develop a standard liturgy anyway, my preference is that they would be exposed to a variety of practices and traditions that reminds them they are connected to a big-*C* Church that exists outside our own walls. Christians have been wrestling with life together and how to transform themselves and the world for two thousand years! We stand in a line of followers of Jesus from diverse tra-

---

6. C. Christopher Smith and Jonathan Wilson-Hartgrove, *Slow Church* (Downers Grove, IL: InterVarsity, 2014), 216.

ditions. Surely the Holy Spirit has given them something worth passing down to us.

My hope is that people who participate in our house churches will learn a bit about other small groups of committed believers who changed the world. They will see that their faith connects them to Harriet Tubman and Dietrich Bonhoeffer, Dorothy Day and Saint Francis of Assisi, Martin of Tours and Oscar Romero, Billy Graham, Julian of Norwich, Charles Wesley, Martin Luther King Jr., and Desmond Tutu. When it comes time for communion, I want them to picture all these saints sitting at the table with us and Jesus. We will use their words and their prayers, and readings from their traditions in addition to our own. In this way, I hope our house churches learn perspective on our shared faith. We do not own the gospel, and it did not come straight from Jesus to us.

A Sample Order of Worship

I'll use the house church that meets in my home as an example. We usually meet for about an hour and fifteen minutes. For the first ten or fifteen minutes, we gather, talk, and eat biscuits and drink coffee in the dining room. People mingle and talk. Families with small children will take them upstairs to our classroom where there is childcare, while older children are encouraged to stay downstairs. At some point, we move into the living room and sit in something resembling concentric circles, with some sitting on the floor or stairs.

Someone asks for volunteers to read scripture and lead the liturgy for our structured time together. Sometimes this might simply be a communion liturgy, with space for Bible study and conversation. We often use the written devotional *Common Prayer: A Liturgy for Ordinary Radicals*,[7] which is a year-long series of readings written from a social justice and "new monastic" perspective. Sometimes we use liturgies from hymnals or a custom-made liturgy. We'll sing a song or two as well.

---

7. *Common Prayer* frequently references saints from Christian history, historical events of concern for social justice, and perspectives from the global church in other cultures. This fits with my emphasis on acknowledging the breadth of Christian history. See Claiborne, Wilson-Hartgrove, and Okoro, *Common Prayer: A Liturgy for Ordinary Radicals*.

Chapter 5

After we read the scriptures for the day, we pray together for ourselves, our community, and our world. There is an open "lifting up prayer concerns and celebrations" time, and after each concern or celebration we all say, "Lord, hear our prayer." We conclude with the Lord's Prayer. We follow this with a message and discussion. The message may be simply a series of questions and conversation about the scriptures, or it may look more like a lesson or sermon followed by discussion. Occasionally we will include contemplative prayer and meditation, or some other devotional practice that is appropriate for the theme for the day.

We segue into Holy Communion and conclude with a benediction we all say together. In our denomination, clergy are supposed to officiate the sacraments, but even here there are participatory ways to do sacraments that reduce the lay/clergy distinction. For example, a church might break the liturgy into left-side and right-side call-and-response, instead of the typical "leader" and "people" distinction. If we appoint people to break the bread and lift the cup, it can be a simple way for the congregation to participate in the drama of worship.

Afterward, we share announcements and business particular to that house church, which might be discussing what we would bring to next week's potluck, or inviting participants to plant trees next Saturday at the park, or organizing meals and clothes for a family in need. Since our people are active in organizations outside of the church, we also share other community events and service projects we are involved in, because the church is not about inviting people to come to our events, but about getting our people out in the world. Some of our members are active in politics and community organizing, so they might invite people to the city council meeting. Others may be involved in a community band or the local film festival, so they invite people to concerts and movie screenings.

This announcement portion is important. I've been in ministry long enough to take part in many discussions about the contentious "announcement time" in legacy churches. Should we do announcements at the beginning of worship, when people are paying attention, and risk boring newcomers and conveying to them that our main activities outside of worship are meetings and more stuff for them to do? Or should we place them at the end when nobody is paying attention and preparing to leave? Or should we not do announcements at all and simply put them on the screen or in the bulletin? If we consider our work outside the walls of the house as our true Christian vocation, then discussion of that work becomes part of worship as well.

A Further Word on Worship Participation

In order to respond to climate change and bear witness to God's Word in Creation, our church led a tree-planting ceremony at a city-owned cemetery. This was both a service project and a worship event. We blessed the trees we planted and created a liturgy. The scripted part of the service featured scripture, responsive reading, and prayer.

But we made it clear that planting the trees was an *act of worship*. We wrote a short, three-sentence prayer that our planting teams could say for the tree they planted. We then regrouped to talk about our experience and close with a benediction.

Toward the end of the planting portion, I walked around to check in with pairs to see if they were finished planting their trees. I saw a father-daughter team walking back, holding hands. They paused, and this precocious fourth-grader held a branch of a sapling between her thumb and forefinger, closed her eyes, and prayed.

Later, the father told me how much this moved him: "I don't know what it was . . . but it felt so much more spiritual to listen to her pray for that tree than it usually does for me to pray for people. It just hit me that there is absolutely nothing I can do to make that tree grow. It's all in God's hands."

I believe one of the reasons New Age practices have become so popular among people, both Christian and non-Christian, is that laypeople are given the tools to feel like participants instead of spectators in their spiritual lives. They connect their lives with the life of the earth, recognizing how deeply interconnected we are. They overcome the way modern culture has alienated us from the agrarian biblical cycles of nature, of planting and harvest. People use spells or tarot or forms of divination because these are not practices controlled by professional clergy or worship staff.

These are forms of "folk religion" that do not need or ask for institutional approval. While some Christians are threatened by these practices and connect them to demonic influence, I simply see them as evidence of how institutional spirituality has alienated people.

There are Christians who lump praying for trees into this category. Some of them expressed their disapproval when they learned about our tree-planting event, which seemed too pagan for them. I don't really care. Giving people a way to connect to the web of life, engage climate change spiritually, and encounter God in God's good creation illustrates the kind of thing house churches can do that legacy churches often cannot. Putting the spiritual tools into people's hands to let them worship most authentically is what we do.

Summary

It's important to give participants a sense that worship is a natural part of our God-given humanity, that something within us is called to give God glory. Giving members a sense of the history and depth of worship in Christian tradition will help them be more open to trying new things in worship, especially if that means letting go of some of their legacy church expectations.

While there is no one-size-fits-all style of worship, something that allows people to participate without immediately throwing them into the deep end of the pool and expecting them to extemporize prayers is helpful. A simple devotional can help a group get off the ground and makes it easy to replicate when it is time to start a new group.

Participation is key. In everything, there should be a no-pressure invitation to take part in the group experience. Folks who are given the spiritual tools to build the group will step into leadership and get the most out of what God is offering them through the house church.

CHAPTER 6
DISCIPLESHIP AND LEADERSHIP DEVELOPMENT IN HOUSE CHURCHES

Discipleship Alone and Together

"We are students of the Way, being saved together." This is a one-sentence summary of discipleship in house churches. Salvation is not just a one-time event, but a life process. And it's not just about getting an individual soul into heaven, but connecting them to a being-saved community. This view of salvation connects the individual to the group, and discipleship in house churches to the bigger picture of what God is doing in the world.

One of the greatest strengths of house churches is that they are excellent environments for discipleship. There is a reason Jesus chose twelve disciples, beyond its symbolic meaning in Israel's history: twelve students is about the ideal class size. If everyone has an opportunity to speak for five minutes about what is most important to them, it takes about an hour. It's also a good number of bodies to cram into an average-sized living room.

After a new house church establishes its pattern of worship, creating a plan for discipleship is the next priority. This is what sustains the house church. The practices we establish determine the life of the group: how we learn together, what we learn together, how we grow spiritually, how we live together as a community, how each individual relates to the community, and how we understand God's transforming, saving power in our lives. Discipleship is one of the greatest strengths of house churches, but it is also the area that requires the greatest time and attention.

When we say the phrase "the disciples" we think of them as a group, as in "Jesus and the disciples" or "He sat down and his disciples came to him" (Matthew 5:1). Yet when we talk about discipleship in the modern church, we almost always revert to imagining an individual learner and how they "ought" to follow Jesus. The word *discipleship* in conventional usage tends to be shorthand for training individual Christians to be better Christians, just as *stewardship* tends to be shorthand for fundraising. We often view discipleship through an individualistic lens instead of understanding that it means being part of a community of practice.

Instead of thinking only in terms of the formation of individual disciples, I encourage house church leaders to think of discipleship as discipling a community. By viewing disciples both as individuals and as a community, we can get a binocular vision of discipleship in the church. We are disciples both alone and together.

Disciples Have a Teacher

The word *disciple* means student. Jesus had disciples because he was a teacher. At the Resurrection, when Mary recognizes Jesus (John 20:16), the first word out of her mouth is *Rabboni!*—Teacher.

There are many ways of understanding how God reconciles human beings to God through Jesus Christ. These are called atonement theories. One that has fallen out of favor among many evangelical Protestants is the "Moral Exemplar" or "Great Teacher" theory. Evangelicals have often preferred talking about the way Jesus pays the price for our sin or serves as a substitute sacrifice for us. Some have rejected the moral exemplar theory of the atonement altogether because it turns Jesus into "just a teacher," like Buddha or other non-Christian moral exemplars. To them, Christian distinctiveness depends on Jesus being "more than a teacher."

While I understand the theological thinking behind this rejection, I can't help feeling this does a disservice to teachers. I have heard more than a few people say, "A teacher saved my life." Sometimes they were someone raised in an abusive home, or in poverty, or who was bullied at school. They struggled with self-worth but overcame impossible circumstances because a teacher believed in them. Teachers can and do save.

Regardless of whether or not you believe in the salvific power of teaching, Jesus's followers related to him as a teacher both before and *after* his resurrection. When two disciples met with him in Emmaus and broke bread (a very house-church-like experience!), they marveled at the way their hearts burned within them while Jesus taught them (Luke 24:13-35). When Jesus later appears to the rest of the disciples, he opens their minds to understand the scriptures (Luke 24:45), again in a gathering very reminiscent of a house church.

Discipleship, then, is key to our identity as followers of Jesus. While we may call Jesus *Lord*, he does not call us *servants*, but friends and disciples (John 15:8, 15). Our leader abandons hierarchy in order to raise up friends.

The New Testament model of the teacher-student relationship is not the hierarchical factory model of education that dominated the twentieth century. That old model was of an expert dispensing knowledge to empty-headed recipients in classrooms segregated by age level and subject. Instead, education in the New Testament model is an intergenerational community built around a set of shared practices where we are all co-learners with one Master. "You have one teacher," Jesus says in Matthew 23:8, "and all of you are [siblings]." Through repetition and discipline, we make ourselves available to be shaped by grace into his image.

Factory models of education are about institutional stability. Our national educational policies are focused on training a future workforce and giving young workers skills for the job market. These are necessary parts of education, to be sure, but this focus sometimes means we indoctrinate young people into being obedient citizens and passive consumers. In school, two of the first things we teach students are to stand in line and raise their hands to talk.

Chapter 6

By contrast, the kind of education Jesus offers disrupts the status quo. His disciples went on to spend time in prison, start riots, and "turn the world upside-down" (Acts 17:6, paraphrased).[1] These students of Jesus, who continued practicing the Way of Love, willingly got arrested and went to prison on more than one occasion. Put another way: this kind of learning is not so much about *inform*ation (gaining skills and head knowledge) or conformation (to the world and society), as *transform*ation, both of self and of society.

In New Testament terms, disciple or student does not mean one who thinks or believes the right things, but one who acts and loves like Jesus. Before it was called "Christianity," followers of Jesus simply called their new way of living "the Way" (Acts 9:2). Jesus said he was "the way" (John 14:6). I tell folks that we are students of The Way, or students of The Way of Love; love of God and love of neighbor. The way of discipleship is to become not better *knowers*, but better *lovers*.

Practices, Not Programs

In a legacy church, there are many programs focused on discipleship, or what kinds of things people need to do or learn to grow spiritually in their journey with Jesus. These may include Bible studies or classes on history and doctrine; prayer, Bible reading, and devotional habits; acts of service; discovering spiritual gifts; and so on. The biggest difference between the way a legacy church and house church approaches discipleship has to do with the fact that discipleship works primarily through *practices*, not *programs*.

In a legacy church, you may go to worship on Sunday and hear a sermon, but discipleship will usually happen through midweek classes, small groups, and Bible studies. Some smaller percentage, the most dedicated members, will show up on Sunday or Wednesday nights, or volunteer for some kind of mentoring. At large churches, there may be a menu of activi-

---

1. The kinds of students Jesus produces would resonate with bell hooks and Paolo Freire. See bell hooks, *Teaching to Transgress: Education as the Practice of Freedom* (New York: Routledge, 1994). See also Paulo Freire, *Pedagogy of the Oppressed*, 30th anniversary ed. (New York: Continuum, 2000).

ties to choose from: marriage enrichment or parenting classes, book clubs, or affinity groups.

In a house church, there are fewer programs. If you do have "extracurricular" small groups that meet outside of the main worship time, they can certainly focus on a particular area, but most of your discipleship action happens as the community does life together. While legacy churches with a large program staff may have an evangelism coordinator, pastor of missions, adult and children's education staff, and so on, house churches do not have such specialized programs. For this reason, it is vital to develop two perspectives on discipleship: (1) a discipleship model for the church as a whole, which answers the question, "what does a community of discipleship look like?" and (2) a path for the spiritual growth of an individual believer, which addresses the question, "how do I get there?"

A Sample Discipleship Model for the Whole Church

Saint Junia house churches use a model of discipleship that has five areas of practice. I've borrowed some of this from the concept of Covenant Discipleship Groups,[2] but need to point out the difference between house churches and covenant discipleship (CD) groups: one is a worshiping community and the other is a group for accountability and discipleship.

The five areas are taken from biblical and historical sources. The biblical sources are

The Great Commandment: to love God with our whole heart, being, mind, and strength, and to love our neighbors as ourselves. (Mark 12:30-31)

The Great Commission: to go into the world, teaching, baptizing, and making disciples. (Matthew 28:19-20)

The Great Requirement: to do justice, love kindness, and walk humbly with God. (Micah 6:8)

---

2. See Steven W. Manskar, *Disciples Making Disciples: A Guide for Covenant Discipleship Groups* (Nashville: Discipleship Resources, 2016).

The historical source is John Wesley's General Rule for Methodist Societies. In order to learn how to love people and love God, Wesley came up with three principles: do no harm, do good, and stay in love with God through devotional and worship practices.[3]

The five areas model helps our whole church clarify what we're after when we commit to following the Way of Love (see figure 2). In this model, we commit to loving God and loving our neighbors (the vertical axis). We also commit to doing works of love both as individuals and as a community (the horizontal axis). The way we love God as a community is through public worship, while loving God as an individual means acts of devotion. Loving neighbors as an individual means doing works of compassion, while loving neighbors as a community means doing works of justice.

These four areas we share with the model used by Covenant Discipleship Groups. But we also add a fifth: witness. Although church culture usually thinks of witness as telling people about Jesus, the *first* meaning of witness is to *see* or *observe*. The second meaning of witness is to tell. If we emphasize the observing part of witness, it means we have to listen and ask questions more than we talk. We witness when we encounter stories in worship, as we hear the Word read and proclaimed. We witness in devotion as we read scripture and reflect on God's action in our lives. We witness in compassion when we meet Christ in our neighbors through acts of service. And we witness in justice when we live out our calling as a prophetic community. I tell my congregation that these areas are like four chambers of the human heart, with witness being the blood that flows through worship, devotion, compassion, and justice. The stories we hear and tell, the relationships we form through story, all empower the work of the whole body through the power of the Holy Spirit. Our witness, what we observe about the universe and the story we tell, shapes our identity in Christ.

---

3. See Job, *Three Simple Rules*.

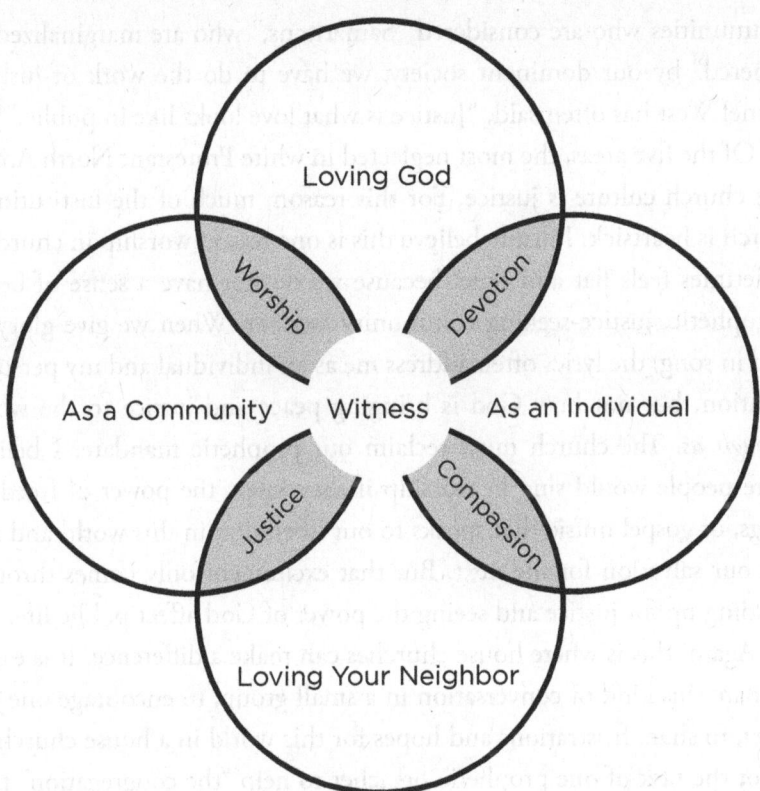

This individual/community distinction is one we often fail to make in North American Christianity. Our worldview is typically individualistic and focused on personal salvation. For this reason, church curricula are written about helping individuals to be better pray-ers, givers, Bible readers, servants, and stewards. It is not often addressed to the church as a whole.

We have a social and communal side to our lives that defines our identity: which tribes we belong to, where our loyalties lie, who we consider "in" and "out." The Way of Jesus requires us to acknowledge that while we may belong to or identify with certain groups, God calls us to larger and more expansive definitions of "neighbor" and "self." Jesus demonstrates this clearly over and over again, but especially in the parable of the good samaritan (Luke 10:25-37), where he makes a Samaritan the hero of his story. If my *ekklesia*, my called-out community, is going to show love to communities who are considered "Samaritans," who are marginalized or "othered" by our dominant society, we have to do the work of justice. Cornel West has often said, "Justice is what love looks like in public."[4]

Of the five areas, the most neglected in white Protestant North American church culture is justice. For this reason, much of the institutional church is heartsick. I firmly believe this is one reason worship in churches sometimes feels flat and stale, because we do not have a sense of being a prophetic, justice-seeking community *together*. When we give glory to God in song, the lyrics often address me as an individual and my personal salvation, but not how God is bringing peace and justice to the world *through us*. The church must reclaim our prophetic mandate. I believe more people would sing in worship if they knew the power of freedom songs, of gospel music that speaks to our liberation in this world and not just our salvation for the next. But that excitement only comes through standing up for justice and seeing the power of God affect public life.

Again, this is where house churches can make a difference. It is easier to share this kind of conversation in a small group, to encourage one another, to share frustrations and hopes for this world in a house church. It is not the task of one prophetic preacher to help "the congregation" take justice more seriously, but of the community as a whole figuring out how to *love people in public in practical ways*. This pushes us beyond sentimental notions of what "loving your neighbor" looks like and challenges us to ask, "What are you actually willing to do? When your neighbor is being systematically hurt or oppressed, do you have skin in the game?" These are hard, life-giving conversations that house churches can have.

I offer this five-area model as an example. Whatever model of discipleship you choose to use, the key to making it work for any given house church is its simplicity and ability to be replicated. The graphic we use certainly helps people remember, but even if they only remember "Love God, Love Neighbor," they can extrapolate the rest. At least once a year, we try to spend some time explicitly talking about our model of discipleship.

---

4. Ashley McKinless, "Cornel West and Robert P. George on Christian Love in the Public Square," *America Magazine* (March 8, 2019), https://www.americamagazine.org/politics-society/2019/03/08/cornel-west-and-robert-p-george-christian-love-public-square.

For those who join house churches because we reject the rigid hierarchies of institutional churches, this kind of model might seem superfluous. Why have a curriculum at all? Why not just read the Bible and follow the leading of the Spirit?

If that works for you, great. I prefer to be explicit about what I think God is asking of us as disciples, how I want to be held accountable, and how I think about teaching others to follow Jesus. I want to be able to summarize in a visual way what discipleship *looks* like. The main issue for house churches is that without programs and a professional staff to oversee all the various areas of discipleship, the task of co-learning falls on all of us. We all have to wrestle with what discipleship looks like. A visual certainly helps.

This shared responsibility is both an asset and a liability! It can be easy for a house church to neglect one area or the other. A group of introverts might love devotional practices, but fail to stretch themselves to serve or share their faith. A group of service-minded folks who only value hands-on ministry might neglect the care of their souls. A group of activist justice-seekers might focus so much on changing the world that they burn out because they haven't connected to the power of the Holy Spirit through worship and devotion. Good teachers know to strike a balance between affirming people's strengths and inviting them to stretch in areas they are weak. If we are going to be a community of discipleship, we all need to be thinking about how we teach.

A Pathway for Individual Discipleship

In a large legacy church, you might have a way to track what classes members have taken. You might include "member assimilation" for people who have just joined, basic Bible literacy classes for new believers, and deeper dives into Christian spirituality for your church veterans.

The problem with these programmatic approaches is that they do not address the individual's sense of self. Even if your educational staff has a sense that every individual passes through stages of faith and that these persons' worldview and consciousness shifts over time, it is difficult to design curricula for this moving target. For this reason, many churches focus on the basic "whats" of faith: what to do, what to believe. These questions are important, but they leave disciples floundering at an adolescent stage of faith development and identity. When the institutional church does address identity, we tend to address it in a static way: "Who *am* I?" Institutions want people to develop loyalty, to identify with our tribe, our church; to locate themselves within our fold.

"Who am I *becoming*?" and "How do I get there?" are more difficult questions, and more threatening to institutional stability. When people have deeply meaningful encounters with God or transformational experiences that are not (1) conversion and baptism; (2) marriage, death, and grief; or (3) mission and evangelism, institutional forms of church often don't have much to say to them. Christian experiences that do not directly relate to more participation in church-related activities don't seem to register. David Benner identifies some of these invitations to spiritual awakening: near-death experiences, psychological symptoms or inner struggles, dreams, listening to our bodies, or experiences of conscious love.[5]

Sometimes, churches even discourage spiritual growth. Benner describes an experience common to many who have left church altogether:

> For years I defined myself by my theology and clutched my beliefs in a manner that represented an idolatrous substitute for God. This led to a good deal of intellectual dishonesty, as I avoided exploring questions and engaging with issues that seemed certain to lead me outside the bounds of orthodoxy and would, I knew, put me in even more tension with my religious community.[6]

Benner describes how our growing understanding of who we are develops over time, which may lead us to question and shed old beliefs and embrace new ones. The answer I provide to "Who am I?" and "Who is God for me?" may be different when I am a teenager, a young adult, and an older person. In churches who jealously guard the boundaries of the religious community, this kind of deepening mysticism and questioning of boundaries may actually be a threat.

---

5. David G. Benner, *Spirituality and the Awakening Self: The Sacred Journey of Transformation* (Grand Rapids: Brazos, 2012), 9–14.

6. Benner, *Spirituality and the Awakening Self*, 109.

Far too easily we settle for holiness rather than wholeness, conformity rather than authenticity, becoming spiritual rather than deeply human, fulfillment rather than transformation, and a journey toward perfection rather than union with God. Far too often we confuse our own spiritual self-improvement tinkerings with the much more radical agenda of the Spirit of God.[7]

This is not simply about churches learning to tolerate beliefs that might deviate slightly from orthodoxy. It's about actively helping people grow spiritually in their understanding of who they are as humans being continually saved, nurtured, sanctified, and transformed by God. It's about making space for mystery, contemplation, silence, and awe. Throughout history, people who have had mystical experiences of God unmediated by the institutional church or by priests have been considered slightly dangerous. Those who didn't get branded heretics and burned at the stake became saints and reformers, like Hildegard of Bingen or Francis of Assisi.

Because the pathway for individual discipleship looks so different for each individual, this is another area where house churches excel. Communities grow *together*. We recognize that we are at different stages of the journey and can celebrate when someone comes to a new understanding of who they are before God.

The individual path of discipleship does not culminate with a list of tasks to do, though it might involve taking on habits or practices that help shape a life. Because this is an evolving process, the community becomes a sounding board, an encourager, and a voice of wisdom for the disciple. How their sense of their growing self fits with the community's commitment to worship, devotion, compassion, justice, and witness will look different for different folks. The important questions for the group to ask its members are "What is God teaching me? Where am I experiencing God? Who am I becoming?" In this encouraging, curious way, house churches can support discipleship as a journey inward and outward, instead of an agenda of increasing busy-ness and participation in extracurricular church activities.

---

7. Benner, *Spirituality and the Awakening Self*, 33.

Chapter 6

Leadership Development

Doing What Needs to Be Done

Here's a quick test of leadership: spontaneously ask for volunteers to read scripture, pray, or to lead music or liturgy in worship.

We do this every week in house churches, because one of the basic tasks of discipleship is to step up when there's a call to do something. House churches facilitate both leadership development and discipleship, because in a smaller group there is more demand for people to lead. In larger churches, I've often heard people cite the 80–20 rule: 20 percent of the congregation does 80 percent of the work. Churches that rely on professional staff often have recruitment programs to help the congregation understand that every member is in ministry.

The 80–20 rule does not apply in house churches: if nobody leads, church doesn't happen. Nearly every regular attender, even the children, leads in some way. When we have twenty or more, we try to avoid having the same folks lead every week. When gatherings are as small as three or four, and one person leads liturgy, one person reads scripture, and one person prays or brings a message, 100 percent of the congregation is doing the work.

Part of this is probably due to selection bias: house churches are not as visible as legacy church buildings, and the people who find them are likely looking for something different. Those who want to grow deeper in their discipleship may be more motivated to seek out alternative forms of Christian community and lead when they find it.

So, every Sunday, I ask for volunteers. Sometimes I'll ask in advance, especially for pray-ers, because not everyone feels comfortable extemporizing a prayer. But if we want to model a culture of doing what needs to be done, we need to ask, publicly, every week. Asking for people to lead liturgy is as much part of the liturgy as the written words. Folks who speak, whether leading the call or participating in the response, are practicing speaking their faith every single week.

When it comes to simple forms of leadership in a church gathering, we recognize that not all people are called to lead in the same way. Some folks have social anxiety and may not feel comfortable reading or leading in worship. They may still be devoted disciples who lead in other ways—by mentoring others one-on-one, for example. A key component of discipleship and leadership is the same: a willingness to do what needs to be done.

It's also important, especially in church life, to acknowledge and lift up the fact that "first followers" are also leaders. Derek Sivers illustrated this in a powerful TED Talk over a decade ago with a video of a guy dancing alone at an outdoor concert.[8] He pointed out that what transformed this lone nut, dancing by himself, into a leader of a massive dance party was the "first follower," the person who first took a risk to join the lone dancer in his exuberant dance.

It takes spiritual strength to be the "first follower," and church—especially house church—is often full of them. The person who risks following makes a leap of faith. Follow a series of these kinds of leaps, and pretty soon you have real spiritual growth! This is one way that leadership development and discipleship are related.

"Disciples" refers to any who are deliberately following Christ and growing in this work. "Leaders" are those who are called, at various times, to lead this community of co-learners in the work. They may lead for a task or for a season, and then step back, but they are always disciples.

Jesus transforms the concept of leadership. In church, a "leader" is not an institutional, hierarchical, sovereign-style ruler, but a servant (Matthew 20:26). A servant-leader is one who (1) does what is necessary, and (2) gets others to join them. That can mean sweeping the floor, preaching, baking a cake, organizing, creating art, or risking arrest at a public protest. As long as they are inviting others into the work, they are a leader. Since God gives us all different gifts and talents, and since we all have different leadership styles, servant-leadership will look different for different folks.

---

8. Filmed February 2010 in Long Beach, CA, TED Video, https://www.ted.com/talks/derek_sivers_how_to_start_a_movement?language=en.

Chapter 6

Spiritual Gifts

Since a house church depends on shared leadership, we're also practicing taking turns as leaders. For the good of the group and for our own spiritual growth, we need to understand how our leadership strengths complement or conflict with one another.

In Saint Junia house churches, every member completes the Gallup StrengthsFinder.[9] We use this instead of a "spiritual gifts" inventory, because it helps us put together work teams whose leadership skills and strengths are complementary. For example, if we have an abundance of dreamers and visionaries on a team, we probably want to make sure we also recruit someone who is task-oriented, who won't let us walk out of the meeting without a timetable and a list of who will be responsible for what.

Knowing our strengths and spiritual gifts helps the church as a whole, of course, but it also helps the individual disciple. People who know their strengths learn to appreciate their uniqueness, their particular contribution to the community, and the care with which God created and formed them. This is part of the self-knowledge that is important for the growing and transforming of the self: I can claim who I am and who God made me to be, even as I stretch myself. Because our weaknesses are often our strengths in disguise, I learn to have compassion for myself when I am weak. I know, for example, that I am not a multitasker. I do one thing at a time. Rather than getting frustrated at the way I can get lost in a project and feel time slip away, I can appreciate that God has blessed me with focus and tenacity.

If I can learn to appreciate myself in this way, it also helps me appreciate others when their idiosyncrasies get under my skin. This is vital in small, intimate groups. If I'm going to be part of a small church, I need to learn to extend grace to others, because it is likely that I am just as annoying to others as they are to me.

Cultivating Holy Habits

I've recently been teaching my son to drive. I found I had difficulty telling him what to do, because so much is kinesthetic knowledge I've ac-

---

9. Tom Rath, *Strengthsfinder 2.0* (New York: Gallup Press, 2007).

quired from decades of experience. It takes mental work for him to pay attention to those things that have become routine for me: turning my head to check my blind spot before merging, tracking the movement of cars in my rearview mirror to guess what they are about to do, or timing my arrival at a traffic light so I don't have to brake and accelerate too much. All these unconscious behaviors are why experienced drivers can get in a car and arrive at their destination with almost no memory of how they got there, and why we sometimes miss an exit (or three) because we are daydreaming about something else. Our brain is always trying to become more efficient at repetitive and boring tasks. Neuroscientists and behaviorists call it "automaticity," and it describes most of our daily behaviors.

It's hard to interrupt these automatic behaviors. For example, I started intermittent fasting a little over a month ago, the kind where you stop eating at 8:00 p.m. and don't eat until noon the next day. I was surprised one morning around 10:00 a.m. to find myself in the kitchen, chips and salsa in hand, with only a vague memory of how I got there. My brain's automatic processes had taken over. At some point, I realized I was hungry, and I acted without ever noticing I had made the decision to get something to eat.

It turns out it is really, really hard to change a habit. Our brains are excellent at creating efficient neural pathways so we don't have to think too hard about something. Our brains delegate certain tasks to be done unconsciously.

When I accidentally broke my fast, it wasn't because I couldn't resist the hunger. I didn't even notice I was hungry at all! Something triggered my snacking behavior, and the part of my brain that was operating on autopilot just executed the behavior I'd learned to do automatically when hungry. The trigger could have been something like boredom, or a particular time of day. My unconscious brain went hunting for the appropriate behavior, and I just did it without thinking about it. Fasting taught me about how resistant we are to change. Fasting is not just about denying a craving or starting a new habit, but also about *noticing* my hunger and *stopping* a habit of eating whenever the heck I want to.

Chapter 6

Even this cursory look at my own behavior makes me realize it is folly to tell an addict to control their behavior with willpower! And it forces me to reflect: as Christians, we often talk about "denying one's self" as if it is simply a matter of resisting bad habits and enculturated prejudices, but it is so much more. When I think about the bad habits of humanity—consuming more than we need, reacting in anger, becoming defensive when we are afraid, isolating ourselves from life-giving community, pursuing short-term gain at the expense of long-term happiness—I can relate. "Original sin" sounds like something dirty or evil, but often it is just our habits confounding our intention to love.

When a pastor encourages people to pray or meditate for five minutes a day, she is not simply asking them to start a new habit. She is asking them to stop the habit of *not* praying and meditating. She's asking them to notice something new, and interrupt an automatic behavior. For example, this is how we might reframe regular prayer and meditation time: instead of reaching for your cellphone when you are bored, begin by noticing the experience of boredom. Once you've noticed your boredom, look for something in your environment to be interested in: the kid in the grocery store aisle, or the bird perched on the wire beside the traffic light. Take a moment to be grateful for them.

That's what it takes to create a new habit: noticing old stimuli and interrupting them, creating new triggers, and following through. A lot. Eventually, with enough follow-through, you create a new habit.

There's a larger lesson in this for people interested in changing the world. If it is hard for me to change a simple habit, how much harder is it for a huge population of people to change their lifestyle? How are we to address big problems, like war and climate change, like our cultural tendency toward violence and punitive justice, if we can hardly change ourselves? How can I presume to change the world, or expect everyone else to change their habits, if I cannot change something as simple as a habit? If I want to change the world, I have to change myself.

And if I want to change myself, if I want God to change me, I can't do it without help. I need folks to help me.

Accountability: A Sanctifying Support Group

In some Christian cultures, our tendency is to use shame and "should" language to change behavior. We put ourselves down if we fail to act like good disciples, and we listen to twenty-minute sermonic lectures on how we ought to behave. The word *preach* is often used with this negative connotation, as in, "Don't preach to me." But these shaming strategies hardly work with children, so why would we expect them to work with adults, whose brains are less plastic and who are far more set in their ways?

If I want to change myself, I must have compassion for myself. Without compassion, I won't have the patience to explore all the complex factors that go into my behavior. Having compassion for ourselves means setting aside the negative self-talk and asking, "Why did I shout at my child instead of paying attention to her?" or "What made it easy for me to neglect praying today?"

Not only do I recognize the need to change myself, I recognize a need to create an infrastructure that supports those changes. And here we run into two problems: (1) This kind of introspection is not something most of us have time or space to do in the workaday world, and (2) it's not something I can do apart from community. Creating a community supportive of change is important if I want to create change. This is part of the desire to create monastic communities.

In her study of the early monastic communities of the desert fathers and mothers, Roberta Bondi points out that the early church made a distinction between temptations and passions:

> To use a clear example: You consistently can hardly make yourself get out of bed in the morning to go to work. Taken at face value, you might want to believe that you are being tempted daily to give in to the passion of laziness to stay home in bed. The truth, however, may very well be something quite different. You may have a soul-crushing job that you are afraid to quit because you fear looking for another one; in this case, your passion has to do with fear of new experiences or fear of financial disaster. . . . Or you may be exhausted because you are not going to bed early enough.[10]

---

10. Roberta Bondi, *To Pray and to Love: Conversations on Prayer with the Early Church* (Minneapolis: Fortress, 1991), 44.

When we hear the phrase "holding each other accountable," we tend to think of a supervisory role, where someone is telling us how we should behave, accusing us of the same negative things we think about ourselves. It reminds us of being judged and found wanting, of social power brought to bear on our human failings: "I don't want to disappoint my friends!" But in a true Christian community of accountability, we choose to be vulnerable in order to let others help us grow spiritually. Often when I share my fears and failings, I find that I'm not alone and other people are far more generous to me than I would be to myself. Being honest allows the Holy Spirit, working through our friends, to sanctify us with compassion, not judgment. It can be a grace-filled moment when someone says to a friend: "You're not lazy. You're afraid. And it's okay to be afraid."

This is one place where house churches excel. House churches turn out to be great laboratories for a group of people working on changing their own behaviors. It is possible, of course, in a legacy church to do a sermon series on prayer and fasting, to get small groups to follow a curriculum, and to encourage people to participate. Savvy churches may even have an online discipleship process that allows people to check in and self-report, or feature testimonies from people who have tried new approaches to stewardship.

In house churches, though, it is possible for people to be part of a "sanctifying support group" in real time. The small size and intimacy encourage people to share their lived experiences of trying new Christian practices. I can share that I've found it hard to forgive someone. I can admit that when I pray, it doesn't feel like my prayers go past the ceiling. Others can offer a supportive ear and wisdom from their own experience.

Cultivating holy habits is one form of discipleship. Habits form our days, our days form our years, and our years form our lives. How we spend our lives is one measure of how we follow Jesus. But if we look only at the habits and not the self, the thing I call *being challenged and transformed* by those habits, we neglect true transformation. Every Christian is on a journey of spiritual transformation.

A *Dojo* and Laboratory for Christian Living

House churches also provide a place for the group as a whole to try "experiments in Christian living." One of my favorite metaphors for this kind of church is a dojo. We usually use the word to refer to a martial arts school, but it literally means "place of the way." It is a place where students imitate a master until the behavior becomes second nature. Mark Scandrette puts it this way:

> We don't enter the kingdom of God merely by thinking about it or listening to one another talk about it. We have to experiment together with how to apply the teachings of Jesus to the details of our lives. In discussions with friends, I began to say, "It seems like what we need is a Jesus dojo—a space where we can work out the vision and teachings of Jesus in real life."[11]

This willingness to experiment is especially important in the church culture of the Southeast United States, where I live. Among some religious folks, there is a high degree of skepticism about anything that is out of the ordinary or violates usual social norms or practices. This includes things like living in intentional community and sharing property in common, or practicing yoga, or embracing nonviolence. Because many Christians lump Eastern religions, New Age practices, Satanism, and the occult into the same category, they can be suspicious of anything like meditation or consciously incorporating the body in prayer. (Until recently, in Alabama, where I live, public school policy forbade teaching yoga or mindfulness meditation.)

But in a house church, it is easy to demonstrate a practice like contemplative prayer, *lectio divina*, walking a labyrinth, or guided meditation as a Christian practice. It may be something as simple as inviting members to take off their shoes when they come into a house, keeping in mind that this is holy ground. Groups can agree to stretch themselves to their level of comfort or discomfort. These classic Christian practices can be introduced in a way that is nonthreatening. House churches also give us the space and

---

11. Mark Scandrette, *Practicing the Way of Jesus: Life Together in the Kingdom of Love* (Downers Grove, IL: InterVarsity, 2011), 15.

place to share stories of our experiences of these practices. I can admit, perhaps, that sitting still to pray doesn't work for me, and I am much more comfortable praying while walking or keeping my hands busy.

Summary

House churches allow us to approach discipleship from both an individual and a group perspective. Not only is each individual learning how to follow Jesus, but we as a *community* are learning how to be a Jesus-following community.

For this reason, it is important to develop a model for what discipleship looks like for the whole group, and an understanding of what discipleship and spiritual growth look like for an individual. Integrating those requires us to consider how the community of co-learners is growing in love of God and neighbor, how we encourage self-examination and accountability, and how the community works as a "sanctifying support group" and a laboratory of Christian practice.

Discipleship is not about an educational curriculum. It is about the life of a community, giving and receiving from the individuals who are its body.

CHAPTER 7
HOUSE CHURCH HOMILETICS

Preaching to Form Community

Dietrich Bonhoeffer says in *Worldly Preaching*, "I preach because the church is there; and I preach that the church may be there."[1] He taught that preaching is sacramental, because by preaching, human words invite the Divine Word to be present, walking among the congregation. The church is wherever the good news is proclaimed.

A recent study from the Pew Research Center[2] indicates that preaching is still the main reason people choose a place of worship. As a church planter and preacher, I'm very aware that most people show up for those first few house church gatherings because they want to hear something I say. I've invited them, and they have arrived as strangers to one another. Something about the proclaimed word has to be compelling enough not only to get people to show up, but to create a community out of these strangers.

Getting people to show up and listen is not the goal; making disciples is. Our objective is to get people not just to listen with rapt attention, but

---

1. Bonhoeffer, *Worldly Preaching*, 112.

2. "Choosing a New Church or House of Worship," Pew Research Center, updated Aug. 23, 2016, http://www.pewforum.org/2016/08/23/choosing-a-new-church-or-house-of-worship/.

Chapter 7

to turn to one another and begin conversations with their neighbors, to absorb the good news and begin to live it. While I or the house church host likely have relationships with most of the people in the room individually, we want them to develop relationships with one another. Part of the aim of the message or sermon is to create an *opportunity for conversation*.

As I pointed out in the chapter on worship, some house churches reject the notion of prepared preaching altogether. The fear is that having an assigned preacher will replicate that clergy/lay hierarchy we are trying to avoid.

In my context, I believe preaching is not only the expected thing, it is theologically necessary. Proclamation begins with the angels' words to the women at the tomb to "go and tell," continues with Jesus's words to the disciples on the road to Emmaus as he opens the meaning of the scriptures to them, and concludes with the Great Commission to spread the good news. Though it doesn't mean that this is the job of clergy, someone has to teach and model the practice of proclamation. And because so many people who are hurt, burned, and turned off to church have experienced abusive, manipulative, and authoritarian preaching, I want to create an opportunity for them to hear the Bible as something that invites their participation and their questions. This is *good* news, not bad news. Proclamation is not something that happens from on high, where the congregation is preached at. Proclamation emerges from the congregation as we gather around the text and encounter God in it.

For me as a preacher, this meant changing the way I structured this time of proclamation. Early on, I found that sermons I wrote that ended with a powerful conclusion or declaration of faith, the kind of sermon that would get shouts of "Amen!" at the end of a legacy church service, fell flat in a house church. Listeners would just blink at me. Perhaps they were moved, and they might even say they appreciated the sermon, but there was a sense that I had said all that needed to be said. Conclusions that wrapped up everything in a neat bow did not leave room for conversation.

When someone preaches a conventional sermon in a house church, it's like watching an expert soccer player do solo drills. It's impressive, but so what? House church sermons need to finish by kicking the ball to the congregation.

This means that the sermon is not over when the preacher stops talking. It means that the preacher has to be skilled at improv, and comfortable with letting the congregation develop the conclusion on the fly. I usually end with a question in mind. I may state the question explicitly, or I may let it be implicit in the conclusion.

History and Strategy of Conversational Preaching

In our house churches, people talk back to the preacher. Preaching in a living room, instead of a pulpit, requires preachers to have a conversational homiletic. "Homiletics" means the theory and art of preaching, but the Greek root, *homiletikos*, actually means a friendly conversation, not a monologue.

The origins of preaching were conversational. In one New Testament story, the author of Acts describes how Paul talks all night long, so long that a young man named Eutychus falls asleep and falls out of a window (Acts 20:9). The word used for Paul's talking is *dialogue*. The church was not passively listening to Paul drone on and on, but engaged in back-and-forth, likely asking questions and making comments. Still, the story should serve as a warning to people who like to talk. Maybe six hours is a bit long?

In recent decades, decentering the preacher has been an ongoing discussion among homiletics scholars. Letty Russell's 1993 *Church in the Round* envisioned a church where voices from the margins became voices at the table. In 1995, John McClure's *Roundtable Pulpit* described a move away from "sovereign-style," hierarchical preaching toward a more participatory, egalitarian style of preaching. He outlined a process for group Bible study that would inform the sermon. Lucy Atkinson Rose's *Sharing the Word* (1997) anticipated the growing postmodern

Chapter 7

suspicion of authority and advocated including voices from the margins in preaching.[3]

Conversational preaching is one way to answer to our culture's growing suspicion of authority, its critique of religious exclusivism, and the awareness of voices at the margins. It takes seriously the theology of the Incarnate Word, who enters our community not as a conqueror, dispensing wisdom and scriptural knowledge from on high, but as a lover and servant. Conversational preaching is an invitation to listen and be heard, and to pick up the threads of a conversation about God's involvement in our lives that is thousands of years old.

In Saint Junia house churches, there is a strong focus on discipleship and participatory leadership. Preaching is not therefore used primarily to persuade nonbelievers to come to a confessional moment, or to teach doctrine to passive students. Instead, preaching in our house churches has two main goals: (1) form community, and (2) model holy conversations people will have at work, school, and in public.

Since our discipleship goals are also about developing leadership, the homiletic method we use needs to be easily replicable, just like everything else. While I appreciate poetic, profound, intricate sermons, I need to be able to teach novice preachers to do quickly what I do.

Structuring a Message

Because I was nurtured and mentored in David Buttrick's *Homiletic*,[4] I still use this approach in house churches. I tell would-be preachers to storyboard their sermon, or to think of it as a series of comic strip panels. Each panel has a single dominant image. Instead of explaining theological ideas, we let the images do the heavy lifting of the sermon. We could also say that each panel (a "move" in Buttrick's language) makes a theological

---

3. Letty M. Russell, *Church in the Round: Feminist Interpretation of the Church* (Louisville: Westminster John Knox, 1993). John S McClure, *The Roundtable Pulpit: Where Leadership and Preaching Meet* (Nashville: Abingdon Press, 1995). Lucy Atkinson Rose, *Sharing the Word: Preaching in the Roundtable Church* (Louisville: Westminster John Knox, 1997). For more discussion of conversational preaching, see also O. Wesley Allen, *The Homiletic of All Believers: A Conversational Approach* (Louisville: Westminster John Knox, 2005).

4. David Buttrick, *Homiletic: Moves and Structures* (Philadelphia: Fortress, 1987).

claim, and when you string the panels together, it should sound like a coherent paragraph. A message winds up being almost a series of snapshots where we explore the theological movements of each image.

In this way, the sermon has a clear direction. We have a starting point and an ending point. The conversational sermon is not aimless: it does not wander from topic to topic, but it has a trajectory and a method. We should wind up in a place that invites the congregation to share their own experiences, to reflect on the text, and to strategize for how this Word of God will influence how we live together as a community.

There are other ways to structure a sermon, of course. We can do expository preaching or narrative preaching. Sermons might be teaching or confessional. But sermons preached in a house church that do not move toward participation will miss an important opportunity.

Scripture itself is a conversation: that's why we have four Gospels, two histories, multiple prophets, two creation stories, and any number of authors who comment on and reinterpret one another. The structure of the sermon aims to recreate this holy conversation within the congregation so that they can take it into the world.

Discussion

Discussion is not simply tacked on to the end of the sermon. Sometimes it precedes the message as well, or emerges in a shift from one idea to another. I'll often ask a framing question before diving into the scripture. In legacy churches, preachers ask rhetorical questions, but in a house church, people answer. Occasionally a response will refocus what I had planned to say onto the needs of the congregation in the moment. More than once we have veered into territory I hadn't anticipated.

Although the sermon has a trajectory, it isn't on rails. This is where improv skills come in handy. The key in group improv is to say, "Yes, and . . ." in response to someone's idea. In the same way, theological insights, experiences, and questions can be woven into the message as it goes along.

Any discussion leader knows that a lively group can almost preach its own sermon on the fly. A quiet group may take more patience and some fishing skill. Leaders need to be patient enough to wait comfortably in silence. It takes actual time for electrochemical connections to be made in people's brains, for synapses to fire, and for listeners to find the words to articulate what they may be wondering, thinking, or feeling.

It also takes skill to keep one or two people from dominating the discussion. There are two critical skills in leading discussion to help keep the conversational ball in play. The first is eye contact. People tend to look at who they are talking to. If a leader becomes aware that discussion has turned into a one- or two-way conversation between the leader and one other person, the leader can simply break eye contact and look at other people in the group. The person talking will almost always turn their eyes to follow where the leader is looking. They begin looking at other people in the group and become aware that they are talking not just to one person, but to a crowd. They may even see other people eager to talk.

The other way to share the conversational ball is simply to say, "Thanks for sharing. Does anyone else have a thought about that?" This simply lets the group know it's their turn to step up.

Sometimes conversations are stellar, and sometimes they drag, just like sermons. Sometimes the message a leader brings and the conversation that follows will both be fantastic, and sometimes one will be on and the other off. But over time, participants are gaining practice at conversation about difficult and meaningful topics that they can also share with friends.

Summary

Preaching in a house church is not the "main event" that it is in legacy churches. But it is no less theologically important, because proclamation of the good news is part of what it means to follow Jesus. The proclamation forms community, but it is not only the leader who proclaims.

We proclaim by creating a table at which many voices are welcomed, and each is inspired, and all preach. Discussion becomes an extension of the Bible itself as we practice speaking with one another in order to speak to the rest of the world.

CHAPTER 8

INTERGENERATIONAL WORSHIP AND CHILDREN IN HOUSE CHURCHES

What Do We Do with the Kids?

*To be Christian is to ask: What can I bring to another?
Not: What do I want that person to know or be?*
—John Westerhoff III[1]

In John Westerhoff's 1976 book *Will Our Children Have Faith?* he laments that the church mimics our secular, industrial-era educational model by creating age-level ministries for Sunday school, and that instead of their faith being formed by discipling communities, children are expected to learn in classrooms. Even worse, he said, is the implicit philosophy of individualistic, hierarchical education.

As I mentioned in the chapter on discipleship, our secular educational system focuses on training workers for employment, not forming citizens for society. We teach kids to stand in line and be obedient to authority. We cut funding for arts, history, and music in order to focus on "practical" STEM skills. Church education, by copying this model, implicitly teaches an individualistic consumer faith. This is the "hidden curriculum,"

---

1. John H. Westerhoff, *Will Our Children Have Faith?* (New York: Seabury Press, 1976), 21.

Chapter 8

regardless of what we intend to teach. Faith formation, Westerhoff argues, is more likely to come from being surrounded by adults in an intergenerational community who do acts of service and justice together, who make Christian ritual and practices an integral part of their lives. That's what I hope for us to create in house churches.

Unless a house church is positively huge, what generally gets called "the children's program" in a legacy church doesn't exist. There is no education building and there is no paid staff to whisk the kids away to Children's Church while the grown-ups do their thing. Because of the interactive nature of house churches, a "Children's Moment" or "Children's Sermon" where kids give their candid input is neither novel nor remarkable. Children can and do speak in worship like everyone else.

But while I'd like to wax rhapsodic about intergenerational worship with children in house churches, the fact is it is hit-or-miss. Some kids take to house church worship easily. Others, especially those coming from legacy churches with children's programs, expect to be entertained and also expect whatever the adults are doing to be boring.

How we incorporate children in worship, or not, depends largely on the choices of each particular house church. Sometimes the demographics of a house church are just weird: we may have an infant and two pre-teens, or half-a-dozen third graders, or stair-step siblings from one family and an only child from another. Our strategy for helping them grow spiritually is a mix of standard discipleship practices, material we create or borrow, and improv.

For house churches with toddlers and younger, we pay a childcare worker to keep them in another room, using a volunteer adult and a baby monitor to maintain safe standards. For kindergarten through third grade, we have an adult volunteer share the Bible story and have discussion and crafts around the text for the day. For kids in fourth or fifth grade or higher elementary grades, we encourage them to be in worship. They might draw or color during the service on the floor or at a nearby table. But they can and do speak up during worship. Preteen and teenage students participate in worship as adults.

Incorporating Elementary Students in Worship

In one of our first houses that had several second- and third-graders, we introduced them to participation in worship by inviting them to set the coffee table, which was our communion table. At the beginning of worship, they brought in a table runner, a chalice of juice, the paten with the bread, an electric candle, and a vase with flowers. We could add tableware or subtract it based on the number of kids we had. They also were eager to help with communion. The biggest problem was preventing squabbles over whose turn it was to serve as helper.

I remember the first time I asked for volunteers to read scripture or lead liturgy and one of our early readers raised her hand. Though her voice was timid and she stumbled over a few words, she read like a pro, and when I thanked her for reading at the end of the service, she beamed. I love having children lead the liturgy or read the scripture. Everyone in the room is pulling for them to succeed; nobody is annoyed when they stumble over words, or if they have to be reminded to speak clearly and loudly. Children's participating reminds us that we are all learners and leaders.

At this particular house church, we do usually send the children downstairs during the message with an adult volunteer who presents to them a similar message and sometimes does a particular craft or multisensory project. This also allows adults to have more adult conversation around the text, especially if it involves something more controversial or disturbing.

Singing remains popular with the kids. Although one of our more adult-oriented house churches opts out of singing entirely (having come from being "done" with church), the children in other house churches learn the simple songs that have become part of our standard repertoire. Some of these include justice and protest songs. After one particular turbulent election in our state, some parents told me about how their kids were singing "I'm Gonna Sit at the Welcome Table" in the back seat of the car while tears streamed down the parents' faces. They shared that's when they knew that the way we were doing church was affecting their children in a way they hadn't experienced before.

Chapter 8

Teenage Students

We are blessed to be part of a cooperative youth ministry shared with like-minded churches. I think this youth ministry is essential in order for there to be more time with nonparental adult mentors, especially from other churches. In this way they get to see that our house churches are part of a broader network, that there are many ways of doing church, and that as they grow they can find a faith home in any number of contexts.

It's also important for the large number of LGBTQ teens that they feel welcome to be in this intimate Christian community and to have a voice. Their faith experience and questions are part of the conversational homiletic that informs our worship practice. Caitlin Ryan of the Family Acceptance Project[2] has shared with faith communities how important it is for long-term well-being for LGBTQ kids to be surrounded with a supportive, nurturing community. Even those who have rejected the church altogether—usually because it first rejected them—know that their parents are part of an accepting community and that there is an extended network of adults who value them.

Adults of Many Generations

When I began church planting, a church-planting mentor shared with us the age distribution rule: most of our church folks would be in a range from ten years younger to five years older than the church planter. He suggested that this is because people in and just below the church planter's age cohort see the pastor as an "older or younger sibling." Those who are just a little older outside of this range tend not to value the pastor's leadership as much, seeing the church planter as a young whippersnapper. Those much younger tend to see the pastor as an out-of-touch authority figure. "Don't trust anyone over thirty" was Jack Weinberg's advice to activists in the 1960s, and we see similar mistrust among generations today—Boomers, Generation X, Millennials, and Generation Z.

---

2. Caitlin Ryan, "Generating a Revolution in Prevention, Wellness and Care for LGBT Children & Youth," *Temple Political & Civil Rights Law Review* 23, no. 2 (2014): 331–44. https://familyproject.sfsu.edu/sites/default/files/Ryanc_Wellness%2CPrevention%20%26%20Care%20for%20LGBT%20Youth-fn.pdf.

But while our average population does cluster around that ten- and five-year bell curve, we have a healthy population of folks much younger and much older. We have retirees as well as college students. This diverse age distribution is, I think, due to the family feel of our house churches. Because we do not have age-level ministries, we are not reinforcing the cultural prejudice that only people in our generation are worth listening to. While many churches capitalize on developing affinity groups, we are deliberately trying to break down the barriers between generations by rejecting narrow notions of who our peers are. Some of our most fiery activists are retirees, and some of our wisest strategists are young adults.

One all-ages theme we've used is the book *Manna and Mercy*, by Daniel Erlander.[3] This is a simple but profound retelling of the Bible story, using hand-written lettering and line-drawn illustrations. I encouraged our adults to color this illustrated book with crayons and colored pencils during worship while we shared "story time." This gave adults a chance to engage other senses. In Protestant worship, our worship practices can become very "talky and thinky," and adults can forget that there are other ways to express their faith.

Summary

Westerhoff's solution to the "Sunday school crisis" of the last century was to emphasize an intergenerational community of Christian ritual and practice. While megachurches create more and more kids' activities as a way to capture families, our strategy is to let multiple generations explore faith together. Meeting in homes facilitates keeping children together with their parents, or at least near them. The sooner we can get them practicing their faith together, the more likely they will be to carry those lessons with them throughout their faith development.

Teenagers and older adults have much to learn from one another, especially in a church context. The actual practice of community becomes the classroom as generations of co-learners disciple one another.

---

3. Daniel Erlander, *Manna and Mercy: A Brief History of God's Unfolding Promise to Mend the Entire Universe* (Minneapolis: Augsburg, 2018), http://www.mannaandmercy.org/.

CHAPTER 9
GROWING THE CHURCH AND SPREADING THE WORD

Evangelism through House Churches

When I started planting a church, I knew that I wanted to reach "the nones and the dones," those who had been turned off to organized religion in general, or to church culture specifically. Although we began as a conventional church plant, we shifted to a house church model about four years ago after we learned that some folks were more likely to accept an invitation to dinner than an invitation to a church building. Since then, our original house churches have given birth to others. So far, the average length of time it takes one of our house churches to birth another (the "gestational period") is about eighteen to twenty-four months.

In attractional legacy churches, we church professionals focus on growing attendance by adding bodies to a worship event. We advertise, come up with relevant sermon series topics, and beg members to invite their neighbors and friends. Growth of 5 percent is considered huge. By contrast, house churches may only add one or two new individuals or families a year, but this represents an enormous percentage increase when multiplied across many house churches.

But the truly impressive percentage growth in house churches happens not when we add bodies to a service, but when we add a whole new house church to our connection. It is not uncommon when we birth a new house church for us to bring in two or three new households at a time, plus a number of other curiosity-seekers and attendees. So although every house church is encouraged to invite and reach new people, adding one or two at a time, new house churches reach far more people at one time.

Churches that are in the evangelical tradition and measure growth by baptisms have noted that house churches have a higher baptism-per-member ratio than conventional churches. In Payne's study of missional house churches, he found that house churches had a member-to-baptism ratio of two-to-one or four-to-one, meaning that each year, for every two or four members, one new believer was baptized.[1]

While I am not a Baptist, and measure conversion and discipleship differently, my own experience bears this out. Our mission, here in the Southeast, is to reach those who have been hurt, burned, and turned off to church. The people I am trying to reach are seldom those who have never heard of Jesus, but rather those who had negative experiences with his followers. In an unscientific survey of fifty people from our house church community, half had been out of church for six months or more before they started attending a house church. One-fifth had attended no church for worship (apart from weddings and funerals) for two years or more. One person who became a host and house church leader had been out of church for five years.

It's important to note that in the Southeast, it is not uncommon to meet Christians who have been baptized multiple times. Sometimes this is because they switched denominations: a person may have been baptized as an infant in the Roman Catholic Church, but their baptism wasn't recognized by their spouse's Baptist church, and so they were baptized again. When they moved and joined the Church of Christ, they may have been baptized yet again. But the conversion they consider the "real" one didn't happen until they recommitted their life in their forties, and the pastor of

---
1. Payne, *Missional House Churches*, 73–75.

the nondenominational church who didn't inquire too much about their faith history was only too happy to baptize them again. This is one reason I don't have much confidence in churches' self-reporting on conversions, baptisms, and how many new believers they have reached for Christ. I've met many people whom several effective evangelists can claim they "won for Christ" three or four times.

Another reason I distrust churches' self-reporting on evangelism is that although I live in one of the most religious states in the nation, and although we have some of the largest and fastest-growing churches in the country, Alabama is hardly a beacon of the Kin-dom of God. Our state's politics demonstrate contempt for the poor, ongoing municipal attempts at racial and class segregation, and hostility to aliens and refugees. Frequently the loudest voices for these policies are Christians. Multiple studies of pornography use show that Bible-belt states consume far more than others. If there is evidence for people who do not know Christ turning from sin and following him in my deeply evangelistic state, it is certainly not from our public life or our private internet behavior.

I've come to see house churches as a potentially vital part of the inevitable sifting and sorting that is happening, and will continue to happen, as denominations and individual churches polarize and split over politics and culture. My own denomination, The United Methodist Church, has become less united over the course of my entire life. Conflict over the inclusion of LGBTQ persons in churches has already had a high human cost. According to research by the Public Religion Research Institute in 2014, one-third of millennials who have left their childhood religion cited anti-gay attitudes as being important in their leaving.[2] This is borne out by hundreds of one-to-one conversations I've had with nones and dones. A frequent question brought up in house church discussion is "What does good news look like in this context?"

While some LGBTQ persons and allies choose to stay and fight for visibility and a place at the table in non-affirming churches, many on

---

2. Daniel Cox, Juhem Navarro-Rivera, and Robert P. Jones, *A Shifting Landscape: A Decade of Change in American Attitudes about Same-Sex Marriage and LGBT Issues*, Public Religion Research Institute (2014), https://www.prri.org/research/2014-lgbt-survey/.

both the right and left are left spiritually homeless as congregations solidify their stances and people realize they or their views are unwelcome in certain contexts. They often do not telegraph their disappointment to their pastors; they simply drop out. This is especially the case for progressive Christians, who tend to abdicate public religion to louder, more strident voices. While in urban areas, LGBTQ-affirming churches are easy to come by, the pickings are slimmer in rural areas, and many folks do not even know alternatives exist. For this reason, I believe house churches may be a viable way to reach folks who might otherwise abandon church altogether.

Since our churches are focused on reaching nones and dones, our theology of affirmation of LGBTQ folks goes hand in hand with our evangelism. One house church we've started is made up primarily of black LGBTQ persons. I have found, in my networking with other house church planters and research into house churches, that our approach is unusual. Both church planters and house church advocates tend to be more conservative or traditionalist. For example, one house church book insists that real biblical house churches need to be run by men, and that those men represent "nonhierarchical" leadership. Others insist house churches are the only truly "early church" way of following Jesus together.

For me, this is not a political concern; it is an evangelical one. I grew up among evangelical Christians who often said, "We're not in competition with the church down the street, but with Satan and his armies!" Though my understanding of evil and hell differs from the evangelists of my childhood, I still believe in that sentiment. It doesn't make sense for someone who believes in the good news of Jesus Christ to insist that there's only one way to be church, or that people need to become like me before they become like Jesus. People who have decided that they are done with church are not going to be won back by doubling down on this kind of self-centered exclusivism.

I want people to know Jesus and be part of a Jesus-following community. I don't really care if they agree with me, because church is about Jesus—not my opinions!

Chapter 9

What You've Heard about Multiplication vs. Addition

If you've talked to anyone about growing church numbers in the last decades, you've probably heard about the importance of *making disciples who make disciples*. We should not be focused on adding people to our group, the thinking goes, but setting free the power of multiplication. We are to be rabbits, not elephants; starfish, not spiders. Reducing the gestational period for churches is one way to speed up the church-planting process. "Simple," "organic," and even "viral" are terms I've heard used to describe this growth strategy.

As I said in chapter 2, I think this is a beautiful idea. But although I believe it, it's not that simple.

First, I need to affirm the truth of the multiplication concept: it's true that disciples make disciples, and I do believe we need to think about faith, leadership development, and church planting in terms of mustard seeds. The kingdom of God is supposed to grow more like yeast, kudzu, or dandelions than like cedar trees. We Jesus-followers should spread like a contagious disease. While "attractional" churches focus on adding people to an event, "missional" churches focus on sending people out to transform the world and multiply disciples. This is the beautiful part.

Here's where it gets complicated: we need to disentangle our cultural fascinations and church buzzwords from our theological principles. In our current social moment, "going viral" is the aspiration of every political propagandist and every fame-seeking YouTube star. The church-industrial complex has so thoroughly bought into the theology of "mindshare" and "viral success" that we've lost sight of the equally important concepts of pruning and subtraction. In church planting circles, the theology of success-by-multiplication is pervasive: churches that grow fast are obviously blessed by God for having correct theology and loving Jesus. But how much of this multiplication mind-set is inspired by the gospel, and how much by twenty-first-century capitalism? While I believe the good news is attractive, is it true that popularity is a sign of divine favor?

The story of Pentecost in Acts 2:41 is exciting because three thousand people joined the church on a single day. We talk less about the day Jesus lost thousands of followers. After one particularly offensive sermon, Jesus shrank his entourage from thousands to a dozen. He even worried he might lose his closest disciples (John 6:65-68). He told his followers that the path they chose would not be for everyone (Matthew 7:13-14). Jesus's own ministry gives us several examples of the limited marketability of the idea of "losing your life to save it." Some would-be disciples did not drop their nets to run after Jesus. They found reasons to delay or deny.

I share this reflection on church growth because I often hear house churches lifted up as a multiplication strategy. Although I, along with others who plant house churches, want more people to understand and support house churches, I also fear the way our culture sells *ideas* or *models* as quick fixes. Though I believe in the power of house churches to grow the church, I do not want Christian leaders who are desperate to stave off church decline to see house churches primarily through the lens of growth.

I also think we need to be realistic about the investment of time and energy in recruiting people and adding them as partners to house churches. In a house church, recruitment, discipleship, and member growth are slow and time-intensive. *And there is nothing wrong with that!* House churches offer an invitation to move from "fast church" to "slow church."[3]

All of the Math

One of the most important lessons I've learned in planting and leading house churches is that all of the math is important: addition, multiplication, division, and subtraction.

Addition happens at the level of the individual house church. Since we are trying to reach folks who probably would otherwise not be in church at all, and since we use a community organizing model, one-to-one conversations are essential. As the pastor and church planter, I have multiple one-to-one conversations each week, both with partners (members) of our house church and with others in the community. I ask all our partners to do the same. If we wind up inviting someone to visit one of our house

---

3. See Smith and Wilson-Hartgrove, *Slow Church*.

churches, we do so with the expectation that it may be months—or even more than a year—before that person will follow through and visit. The folks we are trying to reach, the "nones and dones," are just as set in their ways as church folks. Breaking the habit of not attending church, and creating a new habit, is a difficult task.

For example, the house church that meets in my home had a cookout in my back yard several years ago, and we invited several neighbors. This was simply a way to eat and socialize and make a casual, low-pressure invitation for people to check out house church worship on Sunday. *Two years later*, a neighbor family attended Sunday morning worship. This is not uncommon. The invitation cycle to church is not weeks, but months or years. All it takes is some reflection on how hard it is to add a habit in your own life: exercising regularly, or journaling, or making more time for being in nature. For many of us, these are resolutions that are always "something I've been meaning to do." Participating in church is no different.

What has surprised me is how many people find our house churches just because they are looking for something different. Plenty of our new partners come to us by finding us on the internet and simply showing up at one of our house churches. I think because we live in the age of Meetup, Lyft, and Airbnb, young people are especially less reluctant to show up at a stranger's house than in decades prior. For this reason, it's important to have a consistent and updated web presence. We've learned from experience that yard signs also help for people who are looking for the right private residence. Nobody likes knocking on a stranger's door just to find out they are in the wrong place!

Adding one person in a year to a house church of ten people results in 10 percent growth! That level of growth would be huge at a megachurch. If we have multiple house churches, these simple acts of addition can represent huge numbers.

Multiplication happens at the network level. One house church can become two, and two can become four. In our four years of doing house church, two of our house churches have multiplied organically; that is, new partners felt a call to start a new house church in a different location or at a different time. When they split off from their previous home church (division), they recruited one or more households to form a new house church.

People like being part of new things! A multiplying house church has a special opportunity to invite people on board. When we start a new house church, we typically gain a few entirely new households as either the core group or regular attenders. These open up new social networks and connections to new people. There are more people in our social circles whom we may add eventually.

While those house churches are growing organically, I'm still working at recruiting completely new groups of people into our network. Most of our house churches are ones that I've started myself. Sometimes new leaders emerge from networking, and sometimes they seek me out. If I can train new leaders to start new house churches, those leaders can reach nearly a dozen new people by starting a house church.

New house churches are where the big growth comes from. While individual house churches add a few people each year, midwifing a new house church into existence also creates new excitement and momentum.

Division is something we need to take seriously, though. When a house church multiplies organically, it can be a time of celebration. But any gestation or birth has a cost. Sometimes a house church needs to take "maternity leave" after giving up new partners to go and start a new house church. They can experience the separation as a loss of momentum or energy. "We brought these new people in," they may lament, "and now we just send them away?"

I've heard growth-oriented pastors (usually men) speak callously about groups' fears of dividing in order to grow. They ignore the biological principle that reproduction always takes energy, that birth is full of risk and often pain. I think any plan for organic growth reproduction needs to account for maternity leave for house churches that commission and send away leaders of new house churches.

Subtraction is just as much a part of growth as death is part of life. It is tempting, in a small church, to develop a scarcity mind-set. We have so few people that the loss of just one or two hurts us disproportionately. A house church needs to have a clear enough sense of mission and ministry that these inevitable subtractions don't get interpreted as "we must be doing something wrong." As I mentioned above, Jesus lost thousands of followers between the time of his miraculous feeding and when he claimed that he was the Bread of Life that his followers must eat.

Jesus's parable of the sower (Matthew 13:3-9) is a classic example of growth by subtraction. The sower casts a huge amount of seed, and most of it gets crushed, eaten, burned, or strangled. When I think of this parable in terms of planting house churches, it suggests to me that we need to have an attitude of detachment about the "success" or "failure" of planting new ones. We should fling them into unlikely places instead of carefully trying to engineer their success according to our egocentric ways of measuring.

This means preparing ourselves emotionally for loss. The lesson in the analogy of the rabbit and the elephant that we tend to overlook is that although elephants take a long time to reproduce, they also have very long lifespans. Rabbits, though prolific, live brief lives. House churches likewise tend to live fast and die young.

In addition to the natural life-and-death cycle of groups, flinging seed like the sower in Jesus's parable means that some groups will flourish only for a brief time. My experience in the first four years of church planting is that our two-year survival rate is about 50 percent. We can, of course, look at this survival rate as a glass-half-full or glass-half-empty situation, as a failure rate or a success rate of 50 percent. Like any other entrepreneurial venture, the risks are high.

It is important to acknowledge subtraction as part of the math in our arithmetic of growth, because so much of the church growth literature is focused only on multiplication. People who plant house churches need to keep in mind that this process is a marathon, not a sprint, and that subtraction is an inevitable and essential part of growth. Losing individuals from house churches, or losing whole house churches, is part of the process.

Invitation

In addition to weekly worship, I encourage our house churches to plan events to which they would want to invite their friends. This may be as simple as a cookout before or after the usual worship time, or a movie or game night on a different day of the week. The goal is simply to introduce people to one another, to create a low-commitment space in which the concept "house church" can be demystified.

House churches occupy an interesting space that can raise eyebrows from both conventional church folks and from the nones and dones. The questions "Is it a real church? Do you have a real preacher? Is it like a cult?" can be the reaction from both church folks and non-church folks. Letting outsiders see that house church members are just regular people is important.

All growth, of course, comes down to the simple act of invitation. House churches are about hospitality, and the advantage they have over conventional building-centered churches is that an invitation to a dinner table or small gathering is less fraught, in our age, than an invitation to a steeple church. Gathering in a house church feels naturally sacramental, and the act of sharing communion around a real dining table can be profoundly moving for those who have not set foot in a church building in a long time. As one of our partners said recently, "It felt less like going to church, and more like coming home."

Going

In a house church, there is no distinction between missions and evangelism. Doing acts of compassion and acts of justice out in the community are both ways of sharing the good news.

This, too, requires a mind-shift for house church folks. Addressing the needs of the world, for a local megachurch, involves service days where their members wear matching shirts to do service projects in the community. This certainly makes a big visual impact and creates brand recognition for the church, which is great for an attractional church. But the goal for house churches is not more programs or brand recognition. It may mean, as it did for one member, running for elected office. For another, it means doing prison ministry. For another, it means organizing dads at the local school. These do not have to be "official church events" to be the ministry of the church to the world. Servant leadership is not a program or an event, but a lifestyle. Disciples *are* the church—everything they do for their neighbors is ministry!

It is far more important for the house church to be involved in events and organizations that are already in the community, to find where Jesus is moving and join God there. This is church life made manifest in the public sphere. Volunteering at the film festival, canvassing to help people register to vote, tutoring or mentoring at the local school—these are all ways to be in ministry without creating a new structure or program. Ideally, house church members will invite one another to be involved in areas of service. Rather than creating more silo nonprofit ministries in a community, it is far better to lend our efforts to ministries that already exist.

However, finding an area of passion for the whole house church can be a community-building experience and connect a house church with a mission field. There are still unmet needs, and a house church can organize to address them. Because of its smaller scale, a house church probably cannot run a food pantry or create massive new programmatic ministries. But it is more than able to raise money to help a struggling family, or organize a one-off community event. House churches can address the niches missed by larger churches, especially needs that might be controversial or cause consternation in a legacy church.

Summary

Evangelism, mission, and justice are not separate areas of church life. All of them involve spreading good news and transforming lives. We need to balance the exciting potential of house churches to grow and reach new people with the recognition that mustard-weed growth is energy-intensive and slow. It requires all the math—addition, subtraction, multiplication, and division—to grow house churches.

CHAPTER 10
GROUP DYNAMICS IN HOUSE CHURCHES

A Warning

If you are implementing an organically multiplying house church strategy, you are always in church-planting mode. There is no magical time you "arrive" when you are done with planting and can cruise on institutional momentum, when you can breathe a sigh of relief and say, "Thank God we are now institutionally stable! We're done!" No, a house church (or a house church network) is a complex social web full of complex people. People are messy. Relationships are messy. Like the First Church of Pete's Garage, new churches can't escape human frailty.

One thing I've heard from many, many church planters is this: Beware toxic people. Especially if you are trying to create a community that reaches people who have been hurt or burned by church, you need to be aware that "hurt people hurt people." There are folks who will be drawn to new churches because their manipulative, bullying, or predatory behavior wasn't tolerated by the last four churches they left in a huff. There are folks who will be drawn to house churches (as they are to any small church) because they get to be a big fish in a small pond, and they will stymie efforts to reach new people. There are folks who like "small" and "new" as long as it remains small and new. There are folks who feel that proximity to the pastor gives them power they lack in the secular world, and if you prioritize your mission over their personal need, you will become their mortal enemy.

All of this goes with the territory.

Of course, all these characters make regular appearances at established churches, too. But in established legacy churches there is more likely to be size, tradition, or institutional inertia that mitigates their influence. I've come to appreciate that even institutional inertia has some benefits when it comes to toxic people! Organically reproducing house churches can't rely on these factors, so they must develop a healthy culture. A good immune system won't prevent toxic people from finding your church, but it can help resist their influence. Ultimately our goal would be to have the same kind of healing influence as Jesus, so that our *health* would be more contagious than disease we encounter! We want people to be healed by our community.

I have met pastors who have become bitter and hurt themselves because of their encounters with toxic people. In professional clergy circles, we often romanticize the messiness of human relationships, especially when we talk about "meeting Jesus at the margins" without recognizing that the margins also represent the fallout of trauma, abuse, and oppression. In order to do ministry with people who need healing most, we have to think theologically about group dynamics and creating a healthy culture in the congregation.

Dynamics Are about Power

Power is the ability to do work or create change. "Dynamics" is simply a description of how that power operates (from the Greek *dynamis*, power). When we talk about group dynamics, we're talking about who is in charge (formally *and* informally), who wields influence, how people get their psychological and spiritual needs met within the group, who speaks and who is silent, and who feels included or excluded.

Although huge sections of the New Testament are given to describing the *dynamis* of the Holy Spirit, Christians are often reluctant to talk about power—either socially, spiritually, or interpersonally. Once we open the door to talking about power, we also have to become aware of how things like racism, patriarchy, classism, cis-heterosexism, and ableism find their ways into our personal relationships. We have to be honest about things like fear, power-sharing, vulnerability, and healthy boundaries.

The pastor of a house church can uncover some of these dynamics by simply asking some questions: Who speaks up in the group? Whose voice, though it may not be loudest, seems to sway others? What roles do various actors and stakeholders seem to play? How does my presence and absence, my speaking or my choosing to remain silent, affect how the group operates?

Finally, and most important: has this group reached a point where they can operate without me, or with a substitute coach or leader?

This final question is really the goal of all disciple-making leadership. The organic house church movement anticipates a future where professional full-time clergy are increasingly rare. Rather than building big-box retail churches that can support a giant staff, we are doing grassroots community organizing to midwife into existence an ancient-future way of being church together. In order to accomplish this goal, the communities we create are going to need to model spiritual maturity and healthy group dynamics.

Here are just a few principles I use for thinking about healthy group dynamics in house churches:

The dishwasher principle. The one who loads the dishwasher gets to decide how to load the dishwasher. I use this illustration to talk about how married couples (and groups) often create unnecessary conflict. We all may have different opinions about the correct way to load the dishwasher, but if you are the one loading the dishwasher, you get to decide how it gets done. If someone else has strong opinions on how to load the dishwasher, they are free to share their ideas with you, but they are not free to judge you. If they start judging, they can either do the job themselves, or hush. (This could also be called the "no armchair quarterbacks" principle.)

Complaining is helpful; criticism is not. Of the many principles John Gottman shares for making marriage (and other relationships) work, this one is primary: a healthy number of complaints indicates long-term relationship success.[1] People who complain are giving you a gift: they are

---

1. John Mordechai Gottman and Nan Silver, *The Seven Principles for Making Marriage Work*, 1st ed. (New York: Crown, 1999).

helping you make your relationship better. But a complaint is not the same as criticism. A complaint names a specific behavior, names the way it makes you feel, and names a specific action that can improve the relationship. For example: "When you leave your wet towel on the bathroom floor and I have to pick it up, it makes work for me, and I feel frustrated. If you would hang up your towel, it would keep me from having to do more laundry." That is a complaint. A criticism attacks the character of the other person: "Are you too lazy to pick up your towel?"

We are often taught that complaining is bad, but if someone complains to me in an appropriate way, it's because they don't feel they have to walk on eggshells around me. It takes courage to complain, because admitting ways someone else's behavior has hurt you makes you vulnerable. If you complain, you trust that there is enough respect in the group that a complaint will be received and honored. We need to model good complaining in all our relationships in church.

There is no substitute for time. Group dynamics are built on individual relationships—meaning conversations in small groups and one-on-one meetings where we share what's going on in life. In a house church or leadership team meeting, someone may be worried about their finances; someone may have found out their loved one has cancer; someone's child is depressed and struggling in school; someone is hurt and angry because of a church decision that didn't take into account their needs. These private worlds we bring into a church are not secondary to "church business"; they *are* church business. But often they remain hidden while we plan vacation Bible school or stock clothes closets, or make hiring decisions.

It is essential that the congregation embody what we professional clergy often call "pastoral care" for one another. This means meeting together in one-on-one conversation and in small groups, both informally and formally. Although many churches describe themselves as "friendly," Natural Church Development evaluates loving relationships with a very concrete question: "Have you shared a meal or coffee with someone from your church in the past month outside of normal church hours?" Sharing meals and time is sacramental. If we do not spend time with one another uncovering our common self-interest and caring for one another's pain and joy, how can we embody the love of Christ to the world?

Being part of a house church is like having a master class in group dynamics. If there is a concrete gift house churches can offer the wider church at large, it is how to build authentic community and healthy groups.

CHAPTER 11
CONNECTING HOUSE CHURCHES

Different Approaches to Connection

The trend for much of the last few decades in church life was for a church to try to become a one-stop shop for its members. We made church buildings into community centers with gyms, workout rooms, and after-school care and judged our success by how many people spent huge amounts of time on the church campus. But house churches take a different approach: we do not create multiple age-level or specialty programs. This hyper-local approach recognizes that we are not called to be all things to all people, but to incarnate God's reign in and for a specific community. We are one church not because we meet under one roof, but because the one God has called us to incarnate God's love in multiple places and multiple ways.

J. D. Payne describes three kinds of relationships that house churches have to other churches. The first is *isolationist*. These house churches act as islands unto themselves and believe they should have no accountability to any other body. While this is sometimes a stereotyped view of house churches as nascent cults, Payne did not actually find any in his study. This could be, of course, because such churches are simply hard to find. But it could also be because they are extremely rare.

The second kind he describes as *networkers*. These churches act interdependently. They are autonomous and self-governing. He found that the majority of these come together or collaborate with other house churches at least once a year.

The final kind is *denominational*. Payne noted that there was occasional friction between the loose way house churches are organized and the more hierarchical and bureaucratic forms of institutional life in denominations. He notes with hope that more denominational leaders are seeing the value of house churches and recognizing their legitimacy.[1]

I am an ordained pastor in The United Methodist Church, which is certainly an institutional behemoth. But networked house churches are part of my denominational past and, I believe, our trans-denominational future.

Circuit Riding: Back to the Future

Since I pastor a network of house churches, sometimes people ask me, "Do you have multiple churches, or one single church?"

Although people in a legacy church may be socially connected to only a dozen people (in a Sunday school class or Bible study, for example), there is a visible manifestation of the church in "big church" worship. Everyone comes together. It provides a sense of cohesion and togetherness. In that same conventional church, when someone talks about starting a new worship service, a common point of concern is that two worship services will feel like two churches, instead of a unified one.

In a network of house churches, the house church is the main worship event. So when I hear the question "Do you have multiple churches, or one single church?" I translate it this way: how do we maintain a sense that we are part of a movement larger than ourselves?

I wonder again how Paul would have answered this question. In his letters, he speaks about "the church that meets in so-and-so's house." But he also emphasizes that all those churches were part of the same body and the same movement. He shares news and greetings from one house church

---

1. Payne, *Missional House Churches*, 62–64.

to another. What kept these networks of house churches connected was not a building, but (1) a set of beliefs and practices, and (2) a missionary network of traveling apostles and teachers. The main connection between the communities that Paul served was Paul himself.

Methodist connectionalism was built with a similar missional strategy. Bishops appointed ordained elders and licensed pastors as missionaries to new places (a "charge") as the early American colonies expanded westward. Pastors might have two, three, four, or even five churches under their charge. In a five-point charge, a pastor might be with any individual church only once a month. Worship services were often conducted at members' homes, and these members were organized into classes. Some of those early groups bought property and established an institutional presence (church buildings), and that's why, at one point, The Methodist Church had a presence in more counties in America than the post office.

Today, circuit riding in The United Methodist Church has largely become a thing of the past except in multipoint charges in rural ministry.

As I've indicated elsewhere: church planters in more urban and suburban areas are not asked to be circuit riders, connecting multiple communities. They are expected to pick a demographic or community and follow a franchise model that prioritizes acquiring worship space and enough people to support a full-time professional clergyperson at a centralized location. This approach is driven by economics, not by mission. More accurately, church planters are driven by an economics of scarcity. This is why church planters and their funders usually go after "safe" demographics: the people most likely to go to church.

The sociology of geographical space and of travel also impacts how we do ministry. Although people often talk about our society as being "more mobile than ever," the trend is actually moving away from increased mobility. More and more young people are giving up car ownership and do not drive. There may be a corresponding reluctance for people to drive across town for worship, even if that community represents "their people."

For these and other reasons, I believe it's time to take a hard look at circuit riding as an approach to pastoral ministry. I have become an urban circuit rider. But since I can't be in more than one place at once, we've had to look at other ways to help our community stay connected. It's important for the health of the house church network that our people be connected to one another—not just to and through the pastor.

1. Special Events

Most house church networks have occasional large-group events where they try to get their house churches together. Sometimes this happens around a meal or a large worship event. Sometimes this is more of a social gathering, like a special outing to a ball game or a mission project.

In my experience, if you're hoping for a big attendance at these kinds of events, you will be disappointed. House churches are worshiping communities, so it is a big effort to entice people to give up their usual worship event to attend a different one, or to entice them back out of their homes after having already been to worship that week. In this way, house church members are not much different from legacy church members!

Still, special events are how we make memories, mingle with one another, and reach beyond our usual social networks to invite others who may be curious about house churches.

2. Online

Like most of the modern world, we also stay connected online. Our discipleship model decenters the pastor and invites lay participation at our house church worship services. One of my goals is for each house church to be able to meet without me. Sometimes I will prerecord a video that a house church can watch online, or use live-streaming to connect more than one house church so that we are sharing the same message. Laypeople who are good at facilitating then lead the house church in discussion.

One of our house churches is two hours away. I am not able to meet with them in person as often as the others, but they tune in to our live broadcast or use prerecorded video. For leadership team meetings, a representative from their house church uses an online conference call service.

And like other churches, our email newsletter and social media are also important ways we stay connected among house churches. We have an online discussion group that functions as both a prayer list, space to vent or share inspiration, and informal planning space.

3. Cross-Pollination

I encourage our partners (members) to visit other house churches in our network, especially if they cannot make it to their usual house church at their usual time, or if their current house church is taking a break. Some of our members do this naturally—they like going from house to house and being in different contexts. Having even just a handful of people who float from one house church to another helps create a sense of being part of a larger community. When people from different house churches meet at special events, Bible studies, or similar social situations, those who are more connected function as social "nodes" that introduce folks to one another.

It is unrealistic to expect everyone to do this. Some of our folks are more introverted than others, and one of the reasons they prefer house churches is because they don't like spending the emotional energy of meeting new folks. Some also bond to their group and think of it as their church. It is, after all, their primary worshiping community. The downside is that if the host family takes a vacation or has an illness, some folks simply *will not* attend another house church. I've had to learn to accept this reality.

4. Multiplying Leadership

Our network has already grown beyond my ability to attend every service, so we're developing what I believe will be the most important part of helping house churches stay connected: a staff of rotating paid and volunteer pastors and teachers. It's not unusual for a megachurch to have a pastoral staff who share preaching and teaching responsibility, but in a house church network there may not be sufficient resources to sustain many full-time professional clergy. To answer this need, we are developing a team of bi-vocational "tentmaking" pastors.

I foresee these leaders being a mix of official and unofficial pastors and lay leaders working as a team. We believe the mission is too important to limit to professional, seminary-trained and bishop-appointed clergy. The ministry truly belongs to all believers, and we need a diverse range of skill sets to grow the church—many of which are not taught in seminary or licensing school. We have a practical understanding of call and ordination: *all* baptized Christians are called to ministry. Clergy simply have a specialized call to church ministry that is confirmed by the church.

Summary

Connectionalism is not a sentimental desire for everyone in church to know one another. We are connectional because we are all—clergy and laypeople—called to ministry and are most effective in ministry when we work as a team.

House churches are small churches and, like small churches everywhere, can turn inward, forgetting that they are part of a global and millennia-spanning movement. Creating opportunities for them to connect in person, online, and through others is an important part of directing their attention outward.

CHAPTER 12
OIKONOMICS OF HOUSE CHURCHES

Oikos and Economics

It's fitting that the root word for both economics and ecology is the Greek *oikos*, or house. And it's fitting that in talking about house churches, we address both terms—especially since we live in a world where our economic system has caused such devastation to our ecological one.

If we embrace house churches as a kind of intentional community, we can embody a different kind of economics than our surrounding culture. The example set by the New Testament church included believers who were not only remarkably generous, but considered all of their property to belong to the community (Acts 4:32-37).

Some of this seems scary to us Christians in North America. We are taught that self-reliance is a virtue. Dave Ramsey's *Financial Peace* course, taught in thousands of churches, teaches that our career life should be spent working toward having a secure retirement, saving up enough so that we are not reduced to poverty if and when we are unable to work. While he advocates generosity and tithing, Ramsey makes no secret of his disdain for state-sponsored social programs. People in the United States who question whether a job should be a requirement for health care, housing, food, or survival are often dismissed as un-American solicalists.

While I think Ramsey's *Financial Peace* has some good information and wisdom about stewardship and generosity, I find it sad that most churches accept the status quo of capitalism and what it does to our communities. This is illustrated by the fact that some companies pollute the fresh water of our streams, lakes, and rivers to make plastics, and then privatize clean sources of water in order to sell us plastic bottles full of water. Indigenous people who have lived in harmony with nature for thousands of years are evicted because governments sell their "public" land to fossil fuel companies, and these people who formerly enjoyed God's abundance are moved into blighted land and reduced to poverty. These economic and ecological practices do not glorify God, nor are they sustainable.

We throw away more food than could feed all the hungry people in the world. During the housing crisis in the United States, we had more houses sitting empty due to foreclosure than there were homeless people in our country. This cannot be the model for how God intends us to treat God's abundance.

The early church realized the lie that we can ever really own anything—everything we have and everything we are is all gift that gains the most value when it is shared. They rejected the notion of private acquisition at the expense of the community. They shared possessions in common. The early church was not trying to advance a particular economic policy. They did not have the power to do that. What they did have the power to do was to share generously and create an alternative lifestyle, which they did.

It's important to recognize that *money is spiritual*. This is something we talk about in legacy churches usually once a year, during the stewardship campaign, or during a capital campaign when we are raising money for a building. But treating money spiritually is not something we often have the capacity to practice, because our economics are designed to mask this reality. And because we think of our spiritual lives as private, money and how we use it is also private.

Mark Scandrette recommends some "experiments in security" for groups who want to follow the way of Jesus. I think it's important that these don't actually start with money but with something more basic: keeping a gratitude journal, practicing sabbath-keeping, or buying fair trade

Chapter 12

and local. Collecting and giving away or sharing resources are part of this overall spiritual work of recognizing and celebrating God's abundance.[1]

I should point out that this sort of close and collective work is very different from the work I've done as a coordinator for outreach and missions for a large church. Although people at the large legacy church I served were very generous, especially around Easter and Christmas, and although we handed out hundreds of thousands of dollars for charity and justice work every year and did thousands of hours of community service, there is a layer of institutional bureaucracy separating givers from the work their dollars do. Some of this separation is healthy and necessary: people in need are not there to be exploited by givers, and healthy help that empowers those who need help should not involve voyeurism or a self-congratulatory attitude on the part of donors.

But givers often cannot see how economic inequality distorts our relationships. Many of our middle- and upper-class churches see the poor as needy, but do not see themselves as needy. They do not recognize that there is anything the poor could possibly give *them*, any asset the poor could be to their community. It fractures the way we are able to be church together if we do not recognize our common need: that we are all "needy" in some way, that the poverty of the rich can be as debilitating as the poverty of the poor, and that poor people are both called and equipped to be in ministry as well. We tend to walk on eggshells around these issues because some of us have difficulty losing the notion that money is private and people are "deserving" or "undeserving" even as we worship a God of extravagant grace.

We've had some challenging conversations around economic inequality in house churches. Some house churches have members who live in low-income housing who sit beside surgeons and business owners. Diversity of income and life experience, race, gender identity, and sexual orientation all touch on how we understand money, security, and freedom. A woman shares how she is afraid that coming out at work as a lesbian may jeopardize her career, so she cannot put a photo of her family on her desk. A man describes how a family member with addiction steals money from

---

1. Scandrette, *Practicing the Way of Jesus*, 140–49.

him and has made him late on rent. These complex ways that money and power interact become visible in our life together.

Another challenge with giving and stewardship in a legacy church is the pressure to distribute our compassion and justice dollars to many different constituencies. Even a budget of a million dollars can barely budge the problems facing us. Recognizing the vast yawning chasm of need in our communities, and that many of our members have particular passions about particular ministries makes it tempting to simply give a thousand dollars to a thousand ministries. Our influence becomes a mile wide and an inch deep.

One of the blessings of house churches for me has been being able to go deep in generosity, instead of broad. We have put out calls for assistance for someone who was struggling financially and house church members—and some folks who are not members but who read our newsletter—responded heroically. We have given direct assistance in the form of several thousand dollars and wiped out debts, buying people some breathing room, helping them get back into homes or vehicles. Sometimes their stories are known to other members, and sometimes they are not. For those who know, their testimony counts far more than any sermon I can preach on the subject of generosity.

Viability and Sustainability: It's the Economy, Stupid

Before I talk about how house churches can be economically viable or self-sustaining, I need to talk about church economics as a whole, and how our society's economy dictates how we all do ministry.

We all know the church is struggling in North America. Attendance and giving are both down from decades ago.[2] I've heard the narrative of church decline my whole life. But I am skeptical about the reasons preachers and pundits usually offer for the decline of church participation. They usually blame politics and theology for lower attendance and increasing

---

2. Katherine Burgess, "Report: Church Giving Reaches Depression-Era Record Lows," Religion News Service (October 24, 2013), https://religionnews.com/2013/10/24/report-church-giving-reaches-depression-era-record-lows/.

numbers of religiously unaffiliated young adults. Liberals tend to blame the rise of the religious right in America, which has turned young people off organized religion. Conservatives tend to blame pluralism and changing moral norms and say that parents have just failed to give young people the religious education they need.

While both may play a role in individuals' attitudes, these explanations tend to locate the source of big social changes in people's brains. I take a more practical and less individualistic view: I think the decline in church participation has a lot to do with money.

Robert Wuthnow, in his book *After the Baby Boomers*, points out that the strongest predictor of church attendance is whether someone is married and has children.[3] Previous generations married earlier and had more children; many could afford a house on one income, tended to work in the same career their entire lives, and retired with a pension. Today, people marry later (if at all), have fewer children (if any), and are seldom settled in a career or secure in retirement. When I was born, in 1973, the average age of first marriage was twenty-one. Today, it is twenty-nine.

That eight-year delay for marriage makes a tremendous difference. Together with education debt and a lack of economic stability, it creates a situation of extended adolescence, where young adults do not "settle down" and invest in a community—or community organizations—until they are older. Because they have fewer children, there is less incentive to "go back to church" the way their parents did. If they went to church as teenagers, it may be twenty years before it ever occurs to them to return.

As an aside, I'm not a fan of this approach to church life anyway. I wonder what it would be like if church was not a place where young families settle down, but a place where young adults would launch? What if the church was the first place young people went to clarify their values and what they wanted from life before they thought about "settling down"?

Almost twenty years ago, Robert Putnam observed the social effects of these economic effects in his book *Bowling Alone: The Collapse and Revival*

---

3. See Robert Wuthnow, *After the Baby Boomers: How Twenty- and Thirty-Somethings Are Shaping the Future of American Religion* (Princeton, NJ: Princeton University Press, 2007).

of American Communities.[4] It is not just churches that have experienced the effect of declining participation and membership. Every social institution has experienced a similar loss of community, from the Shriners to bowling leagues to the PTA.

In other words, the rise of the church in the last century paralleled the rise of the middle class and the way we grew families. The decline of the church in North America has accompanied stagnating income and growing wealth inequality. We can see a huge overlap between the graph of participation in labor unions and churches since the late 1960s: both represent an almost identical drop. The church has been in decline ever since the real wages of regular Americans stopped rising with GDP. For good and ill, the North American church tied its identity to the white middle class, and so its fortunes have followed the same path.

Our social inequality is reflected in the church. Small churches are closing, unable to maintain ancient buildings built for larger congregations. Meanwhile, megachurches continue to grow even while the total number of Christians in our country declines. Seminaries, like other academic institutions, increasingly rely on part-time faculty who work for low pay and no benefits, and churches likewise cannot afford full-time professional clergy.

I believe all these economic factors affect how and why house churches are increasingly both necessary and viable. We are returning to the kinds of economic inequality found in the Middle Ages and the Roman Empire. People need healthy communities that embody a different kind of economics, a cooperative approach to life that will help us resist the toxic effects of both affluenza and poverty, of consumer culture and economic inequality and segregation.

How House Churches Are Different

To recap, there are several ways growing economic inequality affects how we do church. These include:

---

4. Robert D. Putnam, *Bowling Alone: The Collapse and Revival of American Community* (New York: Simon & Schuster, 2000).

Chapter 12

- the destruction of our environment,

- the segregation and distortion of relationships between middle-class and poor,

- delaying when people start families,

- making it difficult for families to "settle down" and invest in their communities,

- impacting giving and generosity, and

- making full-time seminary-trained clergy more rare.

I don't believe that these economic crises should lead us to throw up our hands in despair. They present an opportunity to reclaim a discipleship-oriented, missional model of church that is disentangled from capitalism. If the church has tied its identity to the white middle class, how can we go about untying it? If the church has become a place where married families "settle down," how can we make it a place where young people or those without kids "launch"? House churches offer one such alternative, but using this model means thinking about ministry and teamwork between house churches and the legacy church differently.

One economic advantage is that unlike a legacy church, house churches do not have to spend upward of 20 or 30 percent of their budget on a building. These savings can lead to more resources to put toward missions and ministry in the community. This is the biggest economic advantage of house churches! With a robust set of practices, instead of programs, money spent on programmatic aspects of church can also be spent on missions.

Staff, though, is another issue. I've been told as a church planter that a conventional church needs about 150 attendees to be economically viable and support a full-time pastor. A house church network's required numbers are not as high, but I would estimate that a house church network still needs about 80–100 active people in order to sustain a full-time clergyperson.

Whether they *should* sustain a full-time clergyperson is another question. It is rare for most house churches to employ a full-time ordained clergy person. In J. D. Payne's study of house churches, only a couple of leaders were employed full time in church work, and both were connected to larger denominations.[5] The majority of house churches, which were not connected to denominations, did not have full-time pastors.

If we are moving toward a different model of ministry, one in which laypeople are more empowered to do ministry, house churches certainly don't need to be spending most of their resources on staff. Clergy in house churches function more like part-time coaches.

As a United Methodist pastor, it became clear to me a couple of years into planting house churches that I was the most expensive piece of our church's budget. My denominational body sets a minimum salary for full-time clergy and requires participation in our health care plan. My health insurance premiums (including family) are exorbitant, because pastors, as a demographic group, are older and not terribly healthy. This makes it nearly impossible for a small house church network to employ a full-time pastor.

What about the Clergy Guild?

This gets to one of the contentious and—to denominational leaders and clergy—frightening aspect of house churches. Professional clergy in mainline denominations are essentially a guild or a union: we have a set of best practices or guild rules, designed both to protect our laypeople from bad clergy, and to protect clergy from toxic churches. If someone has a "Reverend" or "Pastor" title in front of their name, it is in our best interest for them to be people of exceptional character so that clergy do not come into disrepute.

But our guild creates a hierarchy that is generally at odds with the egalitarian culture of house churches, and it is at odds with truly giving ministry away. While I appreciate the clergy guild, our rules make it difficult for clergy and congregations to innovate. With a high price tag for

---

5. Payne, *Missional House Churches*, 99.

professional clergy, it becomes safer for a new church to focus on recruiting settled middle-class or wealthy families with children than on migratory young adults, unmarried folks, or poor folks. Instead of transforming our sinful economy, we replicate it.

Yet most laypeople value higher education and the academy, and they recognize that the church is harmed by pastors who teach bad theology or lack the clinical pastoral skills to counsel parishioners. I do not believe, as some Christians assert, that seminaries reduce pastoral effectiveness. But we do wind up sorting people by class and educational level when we make seminary-level training a requirement for pastoral leadership. Knowing that pastors tend to reach people of similar affinity, we limit our pool of leaders. Again, economics and sociology affect how we do ministry.

We need to promote a new economic model for church leaders.

Churches and the Gig Economy

Anyone who has been following economic and demographic trends recognizes that the "gig economy" has come to the church. In 2014, *The Atlantic* published an article that sums up the situation: "Higher Calling, Lower Wages: The Vanishing of the Middle-Class Clergy."[6]

Pastoral ministry is not exempt from the same economic forces that produced Lyft and Airbnb. Just as rideshare services have decimated the taxicab industry, and both hotels and neighborhood associations struggle to adapt to house-sharing services, the religious industry has new challenges in the religious economy. We are seeing the same pressure in the academy, where part-time adjunct faculty account for half of all teaching positions, and three-quarters of faculty jobs are not tenure-track.[7] Seminaries and churches are not exempt from these economic pressures.

---

6. David R. Wheeler, "Higher Calling, Lower Wages: The Vanishing of the Middle-Class Clergy," *The Atlantic* (July 22, 2014), https://www.theatlantic.com/business/archive/2014/07/higher-calling-lower-wages-the-collapse-of-the-middle-class-clergy/374786/.

7. Danielle Douglas-Gabriel, "'It Keeps You Nice and Disposable': The Plight of Adjunct Professors," *The Washington Post* (February 15, 2019), https://www.washingtonpost.com/local/education/it-keeps-you-nice-and-disposable-the-plight-of-adjunct-professors/2019/02/14/6cd5cbe4-024d-11e9-b5df-5d3874f1ac36_story.html.

I have been semi–bi-vocational. I have supplemented my income as a full-time pastor by writing and by teaching as adjunct faculty. In the words of one of my colleagues, this is a bit like tying two rocks together and hoping they will float! But I suspect the future involves many more tentmaking pastors figuring out, like the congregations they serve, how to live in the gig economy.

All of these are symptoms of growing economic inequality in this new Gilded Age. There are things to lament and celebrate about these changes, but the church needs to understand the weather if it is to sail turbulent seas. In this environment, I believe we need a mind-shift in the way we understand church planting and economic viability.

As long as full-time professional ministry is what we expect of "real pastors," then our criteria for new church success will continue to be, *Can the church support a clergy salary?* This mind-set means churches are less likely to take risks and invest in communities where they are most needed.

My goal is to reach people who are not likely to be in church—often because they are working on Sunday morning—and to organize those communities into a church that can sustain its *ministry*, not necessarily its *pastor*. I believe this means creating a team of smart, entrepreneurial, bi-vocational lay and clergy pastors who function as a team. A part-time pastor can effectively lead two house churches. A network of ten house churches, for example, would need a pastoral staff of four or five pastors. I have not juggled a team this large yet, but we have led as many as six house churches with a team of three.

Making the Numbers Work

Some house church literature is full of biblical arguments about how church leaders "should" or "should not" be paid. Authors point to Paul's tentmaking as support for bi-vocational ministry, or Jesus's statement in Luke 10:4-7 that workers are worthy of their wages. Some make distinctions between elders, pastor-teachers, and apostles. I have my own opinions that have been shaped by my denominational teaching and experience. But most of these arguments involve shoe-horning the Bible's description of the early church into our current understanding of salaries, benefits, honoraria, and market forces. The early church was supposed to be an alternative community, with a completely different understanding of how money works. We know people have to eat. What is healthy, fair, and sustainable is going to depend entirely on context, and how willing a community is to live as an extended family.

Every church I've served, from small to large, survives economically by the skin of their teeth. As people who follow God, we use nearly every penny of the gifts we are given, because we have this radical notion that God will provide for our future if we are faithful in the present.

But budgets only reflect the official economic picture. The fact is that the tight-knit real-life social networks fostered by house churches help people economically in ways that can't be conveyed by a mission budget. And as we move toward more intentional community, we opt out of the Glided Age economic philosophy of our culture. As we share more resources, we witness to God's abundance and witness against the oppressive scarcity mind-set of America. Making house churches work economically is not just about the next year, but about the long-term. Our eyes have to be open to the way our world and our economy are changing, both for individual households and for society as a whole. I believe house churches are a way for us to faithfully proclaim the gospel in a world of growing inequality and environmental crisis.

CHAPTER 13
FUTURE POSSIBILITIES FOR HOUSE CHURCHES

Back to the Future—Again

For the first three hundred years of its existence, the early church did not have any church buildings. The early church had only a vague set of rules for the ordination of clergy, depended heavily on the witness of its laity, and grew like wildfire. We've seen multiple renewal movements in Christianity through history that use the same principles, primarily in homes and among laypeople. Self-replicating, lay-led, clergy-coached house churches are still a viable model for creating new communities of faith. While so many church leaders are chasing institutional stability, we remember that the roots of our faith are in radical disruption.

Missional-thinking Christians have been saying for years that as our culture becomes less Christian, our society begins to resemble more closely the world of the first century, a field ripe for harvest. The future is indeed beginning to look very much like the past.

Breaking Away from Injustice

I have said that I do not believe that house churches are necessarily more faithful or more authentic because they are like the early church. But I do believe they are an important and necessary disruption to church-as-usual. Planting house churches is a way of breaking away from and critiquing the colonizing theology of empire that has dominated Christian thinking for the last century, a way of thinking that is inherently hierarchical and stifling to the Holy Spirit. When people speak nostalgically about church growth in North America in the last century, they are often speaking about a particularly oppressive form of institutional church that benefited from and promoted white flight, white supremacy, and capitalism.

Church planting is a religious business, and its cheerleaders—like me—often talk nostalgically about the early church. But what usually gets left out of the history is that the early church was highly contentious. We can tell even as Luke is writing Acts that his history is being written through a rose-colored filter. I love the way he euphemistically describes Paul and Barnabas arguing with the pro-circumcision faction in Acts 15:2. The Greek says they had "no little debate." Luke invites us to read between the lines: this was verbal fisticuffs, rhetorical war. We can read Paul's Letters, which alternate between cajoling, reprimanding, and soothing ruffled feathers. I suspect the early church was much like the First Church of Pete's Garage, a theological free-for-all, a wild social experiment in which sinful human beings, under the influence of the Holy Spirit, tried to live a radically different life together.

We need to regard our own nostalgia about the church's "Golden Age" in North America with a critical eye. Church planting and church growth in the last century is also the history of redlining, white flight, suburbanization, and corporate capitalism that has undergirded the building of "successful" churches and church buildings. The church-industrial complex grew in suburbs created by white flight, and it pointed to suburban church growth as a sign of God's favor. Growing churches praised their own evangelical brilliance. So when denominational leaders talk of church "decline" from the last century and speak of their desire to "make church great again," they often leave out this history and what it means for the current moment.

I believe house churches provide an opportunity to step outside of and challenge oppressive church structures. If house churches are imbued with the right DNA, they can correct some of the big-C Church's historical and structural racism, sexism, and economic inequality. House churches with practices that uphold liberation can be transformative for the larger Church.

I am not talking about some liberal ideal of "diversity" or "inclusion." While I do think a sign of the kin-dom is people of all races, gender identities, sexual orientations, and class backgrounds worshiping and having dinner together, "diversity" is not the goal. For example, white folks need to recognize that integrated spaces are not necessarily safe or comfortable spaces for non-white folks. "Inclusion" looks different from the perspective of someone in the minority and someone who is used to being in charge. What we need is probably less like "inclusion" and more like "transformation." A member of one house church said, "In my parents' church I'm too gay; in most white progressive churches I'm too black. But here I can be my whole self." House churches provide a place where people can be authentically their whole selves and bring all of who they are to worship. If they are doing truly liberating kin-dom work, their primary concern is not going to be "looking diverse."

House churches that are predominantly white can hold some of the difficult conversations and spiritual revelations that white folks need to have about repenting and transforming their way of being in the world. This is profoundly spiritual and religious work, and it can happen within the context of worship. But it is difficult—if not impossible—to do this in a large public building which is ostensibly "open to everyone." Most (but not all) white churches that are focused on growing big, successful programs avoid these uncomfortable discussions for fear of scaring folks.

House Churches as Disruptors

While there are some big churches who tackle controversial subjects, and some big-church pastors who speak prophetically, the very work of trying to grow commercially successful churches means that the work of justice and social transformation is often left to the passionate fringe. House churches are a tool that can be used to help the larger church rediscover its roots in personal and social transformation. This is why planting a house church network is less like starting a business and more like community organizing. This is not an approach that fits well with attractional modes of advertising, like direct mail or billboards.

Chapter 13

In the first century, pagan temples were the megachurches of the day. They had the religious mass market all sewn up. But by placing Christian worship practices in the home, the early church also placed worship in the domain of women. It's no accident that many of the church leaders named by Paul and Acts were women. We know that churches met in the homes of Nympha and Prisca and Aquila, and that leaders like Chloe and Phoebe had significant clout. In the same way, modern house churches blur the line between professional clergy and lay leadership. Leadership in house churches is less hierarchical and more egalitarian, more like what Letty Russell imagined when she described a feminist "church in the round."

We also know these first-century house churches bucked the cultural trend of social stratification. People who ate at the same table were like members of the same family, and they even claimed that distinctions between Jew and Gentile, slave and free, male and female fell away in their oneness in Christ (Galatians 3:28). Today, it is still more likely that people of different races, economic classes, and social circles will rub elbows at a dining table than in a sanctuary.

House churches also disrupted the economy. Members "shared all things in common." Though house churches are not necessarily communes, there is certainly a greater sense of sharing and intimacy.

I do not mean to suggest house churches are a panacea for all the social ills that afflict the larger church. Meeting in homes still means that we are confronted with the reality of wealth disparity and economic inequality created and sustained by capitalism, sexism, and white supremacy. A house church can be just as much of a social bubble as a conventional church. Toxic, inwardly focused ways of thinking are always a danger.

But the fact that house churches can be rapidly deployed, formed around the indigenous culture, and imbued with good DNA means that they can disrupt church-as-usual with truly transformative lay leadership. It does not require a quarter-million dollars, a full-time professional clergyperson, and a parcel of land to start a church. And in the uncharted waters into which Christianity is sailing, I believe it gives us the power to reach more of our society with good news for all people.

BIBLIOGRAPHY

Alinsky, Saul David. *Rules for Radicals: A Practical Primer for Realistic Radicals*. 1st ed. New York: Random House, 1971.

Allen, O. Wesley. *The Homiletic of All Believers: A Conversational Approach*. Louisville: Westminster John Knox, 2005.

Atkerson, Steve, ed. "Participatory Meetings" in *House Church*. Atlanta: New Testament Reformation Fellowship, 2008.

Belton, Danielle C. "Leaderless or Leader-Ful?" *The Root* (August 10, 2015). https://www.theroot.com/leaderless-or-leader-ful-1790860733.

Benner, David G. *Spirituality and the Awakening Self: The Sacred Journey of Transformation*. Grand Rapids: Brazos, 2012.

Bondi, Roberta. *To Pray and to Love: Conversations on Prayer with the Early Church*. Minneapolis: Fortress, 1991.

Bonhoeffer, Dietrich. *Life Together*. Translated and with an introduction by John W. Doberstein. San Francisco: HarperSanFrancisco, 1993.

———. *Worldly Preaching: Lectures on Homiletics*. New York: Crossroads, 1991.

Brafman, Ori, and Rod A. Beckstrom. *The Starfish and the Spider: The Unstoppable Power of Leaderless Organizations*. New York: Portfolio, 2006.

Brewin, Kester. *Signs of Emergence: A Vision for Church That Is Organic, Networked, Decentralized, Bottom-up, Communal, Flexible, Always Evolving.* Grand Rapids: Baker Books, 2007.

Burgess, Katherine. "Report: Church Giving Reaches Depression-Era Record Lows." Religion News Service. October 24, 2013. https://religionnews.com/2013/10/24/report-church-giving-reaches-depression-era-record-lows/.

Buttrick, David. *Homiletic: Moves and Structures.* Philadelphia: Fortress, 1987.

———. *Speaking Parables: A Homiletic Guide.* 1st ed. Louisville: Westminster John Knox, 2000.

Carruthers, Charlene A. *Unapologetic: A Black, Queer, and Feminist Mandate for Our Movement.* Boston: Beacon, 2018.

"Choosing a New Church or House of Worship." Pew Research Center. August 23, 2016. http://www.pewforum.org/2016/08/23/choosing-a-new-church-or-house-of-worship/.

Claiborne, Shane, Jonathan Wilson-Hartgrove, and Enuma Okoro. *Common Prayer: A Liturgy for Ordinary Radicals.* Grand Rapids: Zondervan, 2010.

Cox, Daniel, Juhem Navarro-Rivera, and Robert P. Jones. *A Shifting Landscape: A Decade of Change in American Attitudes about Same-Sex Marriage and LGBT Issues.* Public Religion Research Institute. 2014. https://www.prri.org/research/2014-lgbt-survey/.

Curry, Andrew. "Gobekli Tepe: The World's First Temple?" *Smithsonian Magazine.* November 2008. https://www.smithsonianmag.com/history/gobekli-tepe-the-worlds-first-temple-83613665/.

Dale, Tony, Felicity Dale, and George Barna. *The Rabbit and the Elephant: Why Small Is the New Big for Today's Church.* Brentwood, TN: Barna, 2009.

Dawn, Marva J. *A Royal Waste of Time: The Splendor of Worshiping God and Being Church for the World.* Grand Rapids: Eerdmans, 1999.

Bibliography

Dostoevsky, F., R. Pevear, and L. Volokhonsky. *The Brothers Karamazov: A Novel in Four Parts with Epilogue*. New York: Farrar, Straus and Giroux, 2002.

Douglas-Gabriel, Danielle. "'It Keeps You Nice and Disposable': The Plight of Adjunct Professors." *The Washington Post*. February 15, 2019. https://www.washingtonpost.com/local/education/it-keeps-you-nice-and-disposable-the-plight-of-adjunct-professors/2019/02/14/6cd5cbe4-024d-11e9-b5df-5d3874f1ac36_story.html.

Erlander, Daniel. *Manna and Mercy: A Brief History of God's Unfolding Promise to Mend the Entire Universe*. Minneapolis: Augsburg, 2018. http://www.mannaandmercy.org/.

Freire, Paulo. *Pedagogy of the Oppressed*. 30th anniversary ed. New York: Continuum, 2000.

Ganz, Marshall. *Organizing: People, Power, Change*. Leading Change Network, 2014. https://d3n8a8pro7vhmx.cloudfront.net/themes/52e6e37401925b6f9f000002/attachments/original/1423171411/Organizers_Handbook.pdf?1423171411.

Gerst-Emerson, Kerstin, and Jayani Jayawardhana. "Loneliness as a Public Health Issue: The Impact of Loneliness on Health Care Utilization among Older Adults." *American Journal of Public Health* 105, no. 5 (2015): 1013–19. https://doi.org/10.2105/AJPH.2014.302427; https://www.ncbi.nlm.nih.gov/pmc/articles/PMC4386514/.

Gottman, John Mordechai, and Nan Silver. *The Seven Principles for Making Marriage Work*. 1st ed. New York: Crown, 1999.

Hirsch, Alan. *The Forgotten Ways: Reactivating the Missional Church*. Grand Rapids: Brazos, 2006.

Hock, Dee. "The Art of Chaordic Leadership." *Leader to Leader Institute*. 2000. http://www.griequity.com/resources/integraltech/GRIBusinessModel/chaordism/hock.html.

hooks, bell. *Teaching to Transgress: Education as the Practice of Freedom*. New York: Routledge, 1994.

Bibliography

Isasi-Díaz, Ada María. *Mujerista Theology: A Theology for the Twenty-First Century*. Maryknoll, NY: Orbis Books, 1996.

Job, Rueben P. *Three Simple Rules: A Wesleyan Way of Living*. Nashville: Abingdon Press, 2007.

Levine, Amy-Jill. *Short Stories by Jesus: The Enigmatic Parables of a Controversial Rabbi*. New York: Harper Collins, 2014.

Manskar, Steven W. *Disciples Making Disciples: A Guide for Covenant Discipleship Groups*. Nashville: Discipleship Resources, 2016.

McClure, John S. *The Roundtable Pulpit: Where Leadership and Preaching Meet*. Nashville: Abingdon Press, 1995.

McCusker, Paul. *The First Church of Pete's Garage*. Quincy, MA: Baker's Plays, 1982.

McFarlan Miller, Emily, and Jack Jenkins. "5 Faith Facts about the Moon Landing: Space Communion and a Prayer League of Its Own." *National Catholic Reporter*. July 20, 2019. https://www.ncronline.org/news/people/5-faith-facts-about-moon-landing-space-communion-and-prayer-league-its-own.

McKinless, Ashley. "Cornel West and Robert P. George on Christian Love in the Public Square." *America Magazine*. March 8, 2019. https://www.americamagazine.org/politics-society/2019/03/08/cornel-west-and-robert-p-george-christian-love-public-square. Accessed January 15, 2020.

McNeal, Reggie. *Missional Renaissance: Changing the Scorecard for the Church*. 1st ed. San Francisco: Jossey-Bass, 2009.

Palmer, Amanda. "The Art of Asking." Filmed February 13, 2013, in Long Beach, CA. TED video, https://www.ted.com/talks/amanda_palmer_the_art_of_asking.

Payne, J. D. *Missional House Churches: Reaching Our Communities with the Gospel*. Downers Grove, IL: InterVarsity, 2007.

Pomeroy, Claire. "Loneliness Is Harmful to Our Nation's Health." *Scientific American*, March 20, 2019. https://blogs.scientificamerican.com/observations/loneliness-is-harmful-to-our-nations-health/.

Putnam, Robert D. *Bowling Alone: The Collapse and Revival of American Community*. New York: Simon & Schuster, 2000.

Rath, Tom. *Strengthsfinder 2.0*. New York: Gallup Press, 2007.

Rose, Lucy Atkinson. *Sharing the Word: Preaching in the Roundtable Church*. Louisville: Westminster John Knox, 1997.

Russell, Letty M. *Church in the Round: Feminist Interpretation of the Church*. Louisville: Westminster John Knox, 1993.

Ryan, Caitlin. "Generating a Revolution in Prevention, Wellness and Care for LGBT Children & Youth." *Temple Political & Civil Rights Law Review* 23, no. 2 (2014): 331–44. https://familyproject.sfsu.edu/sites/default/files/Ryanc_Wellness%2CPrevention%20%26%20Care%20for%20LGBT%20Youth-fn.pdf.

Salvatierra, Alexia. *Faith-Rooted Organizing: Mobilizing the Church in Service to the World*. Downers Grove, IL: InterVarsity, 2014.

Scandrette, Mark. *Practicing the Way of Jesus: Life Together in the Kingdom of Love*. Downers Grove, IL: InterVarsity, 2011.

Sivers, Derek. "How to Start a Movement," filmed February 2010 in Long Beach, CA. TED video, https://www.ted.com/talks/derek_sivers_how_to_start_a_movement?language=en.

Smith, C. Christopher, and Jonathan Wilson-Hartgrove. *Slow Church*. Downers Grove, IL: InterVarsity, 2014.

Smith, Luther. *Intimacy and Mission: Intentional Community as Crucible for Radical Discipleship*. Eugene, OR: Wipf and Stock, 1994.

Tickle, Phyllis. *The Great Emergence: How Christianity Is Changing and Why.* Grand Rapids: Baker Books, 2008.

Viola, Frank. *So You Want to Start a House Church? First-Century Styled Church Planting for Today.* Gainesville, FL: Present Testimony Ministry, 2003.

Westerhoff, John H. *Will Our Children Have Faith?* New York: Seabury Press, 1976.

Wheeler, David R. "Higher Calling, Lower Wages: The Vanishing of the Middle-Class Clergy," *The Atlantic,* July 22, 2014. https://www.theatlantic.com/business/archive/2014/07/higher-calling-lower-wages-the-collapse-of-the-middle-class-clergy/374786/.

Wigger, John H. *American Saint: Francis Asbury and the Methodists.* New York: Oxford University Press, 2009.

Wink, Walter. *Engaging the Powers: Discernment and Resistance in a World of Domination.* Minneapolis: Fortress, 1992.

Wuthnow, Robert. *After the Baby Boomers: How Twenty- and Thirty-Somethings Are Shaping the Future of American Religion.* Princeton, NJ: Princeton University Press, 2007.

CPSIA information can be obtained
at www.ICGtesting.com
Printed in the USA
LVHW030703300720
661886LV00006B/8